Portraits of Community

African American Photography in Texas

Portraits
of Community

African American Photography
in Texas

Alan Govenar

TEXAS STATE HISTORICAL ASSOCIATION / AUSTIN

Library of Congress Cataloging-in-Publication Data
Portraits of community : African American photography in Texas / [compiled] by Alan Govenar.
     p.   cm.
Includes bibliographical references and index.
ISBN 0-87611-153-3 (cloth : acid-free paper)
1. Photography—Texas history—History—Pictorial works. 2. Afro-American photographers—Texas—
Interviews. 3. Afro-Americans—Texas—History—Portraits. 4. Texas—Social life and customs—
Pictorial—works. I. Govenar, Alan B., 1952–   .
TR24.T4P67 1996
779' .9976400496073—dc20   96-12516
                                                                                  CIP

ISBN 0-87611-153-3

10 9 8 7 6 5 4 3 2 1   96 97 98 99 00 01 02 03 04 05

Published by the Texas State Historical Association in cooperation with the Center for Studies in Texas History at the University of Texas at Austin.

All photographs in the book are black-and-white gelatin silver prints, unless otherwise noted.
Frontispiece: Earlie Hudnall Jr., *Lady with Flag, July 4th,* Houston, Texas, 1987. *Courtesy Benteler-Morgan Galleries.*

Designed by David Timmons.

∞
The paper used in this book meets the minimum requirement of the American National Standard for Permanence of Paper for Printed Library Materials, Z39.48—1984.

Contents

Acknowledgments

My work on this book spans more than a decade and has benefited greatly over the years from the assistance of a diverse array of individuals and institutions. Most of all, I have been inspired by the photographers themselves, who shared their vision and instilled in me the determination to persevere.

Rick Stewart, Harry Robinson, Ron Gleason, Tom Southall, Barbara McCandless, Alvia Wardlaw, Anne Tucker, Susan Morgan, Michael Peranteau, Deborah Willis, Bob O'Connor, Jeannette Dixon, Mary Cleveland, Lloyd Thompson, Shirley Hudson, John Slate, John Crain, Monte Youngs, Bill Howze, Ron Tyler, George Ward, Martin Kohout, Janice Pinney, Don Carleton, John Wheat, Betty Baptiste Guy, Genevieve Brembry, Weston Naef, and Bob Ray Sanders challenged me with difficult questions and offered insight as my efforts advanced.

The Board of Documentary Arts has encouraged this undertaking since its inception in 1985. Grants to Documentary Arts from the Texas Commission on the Arts, Texas Committee for the Humanities, National Endowment for the Arts, National Historical Publications and Records Commission, Summerlee Foundation, and Meadows Foundation have nurtured my research and assisted me in organizing the touring exhibition, *Portraits of Community: African American Photography in Texas* and in establishing the Texas African American Photography Collection, Archive, and Internship Program.

The Center for American History at the University of Texas at Austin supported my collection of some oral histories from the photographers. Kimberly Haley-Coleman and Cathy Byrne assisted in the arduous task of interview transcription. My daughter, Breea Govenar, helped with the cataloging of the photographs for publication.

Tracy Glantz and Ron Evans produced the contemporary prints for reproduction when vintage prints were not available and adhered to the style and intent of each photographer. Steven Stappenbeck of the Center for American History and Jim Danky of the State Historical Society of Wisconsin aided me in compiling the appendix listing of African American newspapers and magazines in Texas.

Kaleta Doolin, my wife since 1989, was excited by this endeavor early on, and has been invaluable to me in helping to bring this book to fruition.

Introduction

BACKGROUND

Photographs validate experience and imply importance. They provide visual evidence, but may also deceive the viewer. The process of composition frames the image and alters the context of perception. Thus, photographs can impact the knowledge and understanding of history. This is especially true for culturally specific and minority populations, where accurate documentation has sometimes been limited by prejudice and discrimination.

This book focuses on the growth and development of vernacular and community photography among African Americans in Texas. By definition, vernacular photography is made by individuals for personal use. These photographers generally have no formal training and use simple point-and-shoot cameras to produce snapshots. Community photographers document the world in which they live in a different manner. While they may also have little training, they have a social purpose which usually is financially motivated. They tend to employ professional equipment and make prints to satisfy the needs of the people they serve.

Both vernacular and community photography by African Americans in Texas have received relatively little attention. A history of Texas photography published by Texas Monthly Press, for example, does not include any references to African American photographers.[1] The exclusion of African American photographers is not only apparent in works on Texas history but is, in fact, pervasive in literature on photography in general. The 1982 edition of Beaumont Newhall's *The History of Photography*,[2] the standard text in the field, does not mention one black photographer. Moreover, the catalogue for the seminal exhibition, *A Century of Black Photographers: 1840–1960*, does not include the work of a single Texas photographer, although the names of several are listed in an appendix, with dates and addresses gathered from city directories.[3]

Some of the best-known photographs of African Americans in Texas are those made by white photographers, principally by Erwin Smith during the years 1910–1915 and by Russell Lee and his contemporaries who traveled extensively in the state for the Farm Security Administration in the 1930s and 1940s.[4] These well-crafted images have appeared in numerous publications and have contributed, though perhaps unintentionally, to the stereotyping of African American culture in the state.

When I received a commission from the Dallas Museum of Art in 1984 to produce a book, audio tape, and three films on Texas blues (as part of the *Lone Star Regionalism* exhibition), I traveled around the state to identify the highest-quality photographic documentation of African American music, life, and culture.[5] Through contacts with community leaders and musicians, I encountered a generation of African American photographers whose work had essentially been overlooked by museums and cultural institutions in the state.

In the years since I completed the *Living Texas Blues* project, I have continued to document the lives and careers of those photographers that I met for the first time in 1984. This book presents an historical overview of African American photography in Texas and establishes a solid basis for further study. Many of the photographers included in this book are virtually unknown. Some are in their seventies and eighties and in frail health. This book provides

Erwin E. Smith, *African American Cowboys,* Bonham, Texas, ca. 1910. *Erwin E. Smith Collection of the Library of Congress, on deposit at the Amon Carter Museum, Fort Worth, Texas.*

an opportunity to celebrate these older photographers and to understand them in the context of their antecedents and of their younger peers.

In compiling the book, I engaged in extensive fieldwork, conducting interviews with those photographers who began their careers in the 1930s and 1940s and continued to work in the state. I asked all of the photographers essentially the same set of questions, inquiring about their birth and childhood, family backgrounds, the social conditions in which they lived and worked (including the nature of their community involvement and the impact of segregation, discrimination, and integration), influences in photography, camera and darkroom equipment, printing style, lighting, clientele, and personal philosophy. In so doing, I discovered that their careers and lives defied

broad generalization. Each of the photographers has a distinctive voice and an essentially unique set of experiences that led him or her into photography as a profession or pastime. However, they did not work entirely independent of each other. They shared a common vision of the importance of photography in African American community life that was articulated in the images they created for black newspapers, school yearbooks, and other local publications. Among the photographers represented in this book there was also a tradition of mentorship and connoisseurship. A. C. Teal, for example, had his own private school of photography and was the teacher of Benny Joseph, Elnora Frazier, and Juanita Williams. In addition, Teal traveled around the state as an itinerant photographer and was a mentor to Calvin

Littlejohn in Fort Worth, where he often stayed for weeks to make portraits of many of the prominent black families. Eugene Roquemore was the student of Curtis Humphrey at Wiley College. Earlie Hudnall worked with Herbert Provost in his studio and studied photography with Rodney Evans at Texas Southern University.

As African American theologian James Cone points out, the politics of racial discrimination necessarily created a black reality that is distinctly different from that of whites, and from that reality emerged a distinct black culture.[6] In this context, the role of the black photographer was not only to document but to validate the African American experience. Photography was a means to establish the significance of the interpersonal relations and institutions that were intrinsic to community life.

In editing my interviews with the photographers, I deleted those parts of speech, including hesitations and interruptions, that might impede understanding. My intent was to make their speech fluent in written form and not to alter the grammar and vocabulary.

I grouped the photographers geographically. In this way, the autobiographical texts interweave with the photographs to reveal the matrix of community life. At times, the photographers competed for clientele, while in other instances, especially in the larger urban areas of Dallas and Houston, they divided the vast amount of community work among themselves and shared their resources and expertise. In Dallas, for example, A. B. Bell and Marion Butts were both photographers for the Dallas *Express* newspaper. In Houston, Benny Joseph and Herbert Provost shared a studio; Elnora Frazier worked as a printer for Louise Martin.

To supplement the interviews with the photographers, the book presents additional oral histories that further elaborate the historical

Russell Lee, *Marshall, Texas (vicinity)*, March 1939. *Courtesy Library of Congress.*

Unknown maker, American school, *Seated Child*, Dallas, Texas (?), ca. 1890.

Unknown maker, American school, *Seated Group*, Dallas, Texas (?), ca. 1890–1910.

6

Unknown maker, American school, *Seated Man*, Dallas, Texas (?), ca. 1900–1910.

Powell, *Henry Madison, R. D. Madison's Father*, San Antonio, Texas, ca. 1905.

George Schuwirth, *Lizzie Clark*, Austin, Texas, ca. 1870–1880.

Harper and Company, *Two Children*, Houston, Texas, ca. 1899–1901.

Keystone Stereograph P92 (V226123), Underwood and Underwood Reprint, 1903.

context of their work. These include the widows of Robert Whitby and Eugene Roquemore and the son of Morris Crawford, as well as Ivery Myers (who worked for A. C. Teal), Francis Williams (a prominent civil rights attorney in Houston) and Teresa Sidle Hardeman (a retired antique dealer in Austin).

Hardeman provided me with unidentified tintypes and other early prints that her father purchased from African American families in Central Texas as early as 1915. She speculates that these tintypes date from the period between 1865 to 1880 and were made in white-owned studios on Congress Avenue in Austin. She maintains that "black people couldn't afford cameras and there were no black photographers in Austin at that time. Some of the tintypes were probably the only photographs that these people ever had made of themselves and it's likely they were made for special occasions—weddings, anniversaries, or maybe baptism into the church."[7] However, it is possible that these tintypes were made by black photographers elsewhere in Texas, or that they were brought by people from other places in the South.

While the tintypes can only be identified by the place where I found them, some of the early paper prints are stamped with the name of the photographic studio in which they were made. These studios were, as Hardeman suggests, white-owned and -operated. They include the establishments of John Swartz, William Bryant, and Frank Simpson in Fort Worth; David P. Barr and Charles J. Wright, Clarence C. Deane, and Thomas J. Harper in Houston; Jervis C. Deane in Waco; George Schuwirth in Austin; Alonzo Newell Callaway, Bolton and Mitchell, L. T. Powell, and Lewison Studio in San Antonio; and Anderson Art Studio in Dallas.[8]

These portraits depict African Americans between approximately 1865 and 1910 who appear somewhat prosperous and self-assured. The earliest prints and tintypes, however, are extremely difficult to date precisely. Given the lack of documentation, it is impossible to determine the exact status of the people in the photographs. If the images predate the Emancipation Proclamation or June 19, 1865 (Juneteenth, when the news of the Emancipation Proclamation became public in Texas), the people may or may not have been slaves. Moreover, the couples in the photographs may or may not have been married. The institution of marriage was illegal in slavery, and only in rare instances did slaveholders take their slaves to be photographed.

Some of the tintypes in the book, however, do bear a striking resemblance to those featured in the *Hidden Witness* exhibition, curated by Weston Naef and Jackie Napoleon Wilson.[9] This exhibition featured a stunning array of daguerreotypes, tintypes, and ambrotypes depicting African Americans before, during, and shortly after the Civil War. None of the images in this exhibition, however, were made in Texas, and consequently it is difficult to make any definitive comparisons. Nonetheless, it is clear that emancipation from slavery helped to proliferate photography among and by African Americans.

These portraits of African Americans constitute a sharp contrast to the racial bigotry of stereographs marketed to a white audience during the same period. For example, Keystone stereograph P92 (V26123) shows a black family in front of a log house with a caption that reads, "A Humble but Happy Home down South in Dixie Land." This particular stereograph is a reprint by the Keystone View Company of an image copyrighted by the Underwood and Underwood Company in 1903. However, the text on the back of the stereograph was apparently added by Keystone after it acquired the image from Underwood and Underwood in 1912.[10] The exact source of this stereograph is questionable, since Underwood and Underwood was itself a revival company that did not begin producing stereo views from its own negatives until 1891.

In any event, the back of the stereograph further elaborates the caricatures of African Americans typical of this period: "Perhaps this is a happy home for these children. It is the only kind they know. Maybe it should help us to be happy with what we have. You might think of this picture the next time you ask your mother to give you something you do not need. These little negro children haven't the toys you have, yet they can find something with which to play. They haven't the clothes you have and that doesn't seem to bother them. Perhaps they live in a house without a stove, yet they look as if they had enough to eat. See that wall of stones at the end of their house. It is the chimney and inside is a fireplace where their mother cooks.

This house is made of logs and the cracks are filled with mud. Can you find any windows?

"Many negroes throughout the South are very poor. They even use rope in place of reins for their mule. Sometimes their children grow up without learning to read or write. Uncle Sam does not like this. He wishes all his boys and girls to have a chance to go to school."

Historian Rayford W. Logan has written that "the years bracketed by the administrations of Rutherford B. Hayes and Woodrow Wilson can be called the 'Nadir' of the Negro's post-emancipation history."[11] Despite the harsh realities of Reconstruction and the Jim Crow system of comprehensive segregation that denied blacks the vote, restricted housing and social activities, and excluded them from jobs, a multitude of national African American religious, professional, and social organizations were formed at this time. Historian Michael R. Winston asserts that these organizations established the basis for the emergence of a significant middle class: "Thwarted by the barriers of segregation," Winston writes, "this group provided the critical mass of leadership among black Americans, and offered the professional services of teachers, physicians, dentists, lawyers, and clergymen that were otherwise denied them by white institutions and professionals."[12]

This group of African American professionals and their families employed photographers to make portraits and records of social events. In many instances, as the exhibition *A Century of Black Photography* revealed, the photographers of this emerging middle class were African American themselves, although when black photographers were not available, people patronized the white studios.

HISTORICAL CONTEXT

In Texas there were African American photographers working after the Civil War. The 1866 *Houston City Directory* lists a black woman, Mary Warren, as a photographic printer, although no prints by her have ever been located and she is not listed in subsequent city directories.[13]

The 1900 census records identify seven African American photographers who were at that time working in photography in the state.

Unknown maker, American school, *Seated Woman*, Dallas, Texas (?), ca. 1865–1875.

Unknown maker, American school, *Seated Woman*, Fort Worth, Texas (?), ca. 1870–1880.

Unknown maker, American school, *Seated Woman*, Dallas, Texas (?), ca. 1890.

They include Thomas Banks (b. 1865) in Pearsall, Albert (b. 1891) and Ardell (b. 1877) Beverly in Galveston, Willie Christian (b. 1879) in Galveston, Larry Rogers (b. 1861) in Harrison County, Joe Thomas (b. 1865) in Houston, and Joe Thompson (b. 1865) in Galveston.[14]

Other than this basic census information and the body of undocumented tintypes and prints that I gathered around the state, no evidence of these photographers has been located. It is possible that some were itinerant, or may have worked in the studios of white photographers, or that they changed professions later in life.

The undocumented portraits of African Americans during the late nineteenth century do not differ significantly in style from those made of and by their white counterparts. Generally, the portraits were done in a straight factual style, using undramatic natural lighting with the subjects looking frontally or slightly away from the camera lens.

Nonetheless, these portraits do emphasize the dignity and self-esteem of the subjects. To have such a portrait made was indicative of social status and of success in spite of the adversities of segregation and racism.

Aside from these scattered portraits, however, there are few photographs of the suffering and poverty in which most African Americans lived. Angela Davis, in her catalogue essay for *A Century of Black Photographers,* points out that despite the fact that "the works and careers of the few early black photographers appear entirely removed from the situations and aspirations of the masses of Afro-Americans," black writings of the period are full of bitterly honest accounts of mob violence and lynchings.[15]

In Texas the incidents of racial intimidation and terror were numerous, although little photographic documentation exists. Photographs were apparently not made of the notorious 1906 assault on black soldiers in Brownsville, nor of the May 15, 1916, lynching of Jesse Washington, burned to death in Waco before a cheering crowd of fifteen thousand people.[16] There is, however, a stereograph of the "execution of the negroe Wesly Jones (by 'Hanging') near the Banks of the Trinity River on Friday Aug. 11th 1876" in Dallas. In addition, there are photographs of three "Hanged negroes, possibly the Reddick/ Johnson/ Whitehead lynching

near Boonville, Brazos County, Texas"; of "Henry Smith, or Dowery, the negro fiend who brutally outraged and murdered a 3-year-old girl, [who] was burned at the stake . . . after he had been seared from head to feet with red hot irons," in Paris, Texas, on February 1, 1893, before a mob of more than ten thousand people; and of George Hughes before and after he was hanged and burned to death in Sherman in 1930.[17] In all of these incidents, the photographers are unknown, but the impact is nonetheless horrifying.

There is no evidence to suggest that African American photographers witnessed any lynchings in Texas. However, historian Dannehl Twomey has documented photographs that were made by black photographers in their communities during the period in which lynchings and racial intimidation were rampant in the state.

In 1905 Lucius Harper opened a studio at his residence at 1107 Andrews in Houston. Harper moved to Houston from Galveston, where he had been a photographer since 1899.[18]

Between 1905 and 1927, ten black photographers advertised in the *Houston City Directory,* including Edward M. Robinson, Randolph Brown, Nicholas Broussard, Charles G. Harris, Gertrude Lewis, Seth Fitch, and A. C. Teal.[19] Of these, Harris and Teal were clearly the most prominent.

Harris came to Houston from Little Rock, Arkansas, where he learned his skills as a photographer and operated a studio for six years. In Texas, he began working in the African American community as early as 1909, but did not advertise in the general city directory until 1915, when he was selected as the photographer for the *Red Book of Houston.* Published in 1915, the *Red Book* was devoted to the life and culture of African Americans, and featured sections on education, occupations, health and related areas, and a listing of black businesses and community services.[20] Harris's photographs included portraits of ex-slaves, educators, doctors, lawyers, civic and religious leaders, community groups, and social activities. Interestingly enough, Harris's stamped logo on the back of his prints indicated that his studio was not only his residence but also a hotel.

After 1931, Harris did not advertise in the *Houston City Directory,* and the details of his

Unknown maker, American school, *Lynching*, Paris, Texas, 1893. *CN 03551, Prints and Photographs Collection, Paris, Texas, file. Courtesy Center for American History, University of Texas at Austin.*

Unknown maker, American school, *Lynching (Before)*, Sherman, Texas, 1930. *CN 03113, Roy Wilkinson Aldrich Papers, 1858–1955. Courtesy Center for American History, University of Texas at Austin.*

Unknown maker, American school, *Lynching (After)*, Sherman, Texas, 1930. *CN 03114, Roy Wilkinson Aldrich Papers, 1858–1955. Courtesy Center for American History, University of Texas at Austin.*

Unknown maker, *Charles G. Harris, The Camera Man*, Houston, Texas, 1915. *Courtesy Metropolitan Research Center, Houston Public Library.*

life and death are sketchy. Similarly, little is known about A. C. Teal, although his stature among African American photographers in Texas is legendary. Virtually every photographer interviewed for this book talked about Teal and his importance.

Albert Chester Teal was reportedly born in 1891 in Crockett, Texas, and moved to Houston at an early age.[21] His father was a tinsmith and it is unknown exactly how Teal learned photography. While in his twenties, Teal traveled around Texas as a portraitist and procured contracts for photography in black colleges, as well as in elementary and secondary schools. In Waco, he met his wife-to-be, Elnora, and later taught her photography.

Teal opened his first studio in Houston in 1919 at 1111 Andrews (in the same block where Lucius Harper had a studio from 1905 to 1907), but later moved to 409½ Milam between Preston and Prairie in downtown Houston. By this time, Mrs. Teal had learned photography from her husband, and business for the Teal Studio was flourishing. Mr. Teal opened a second studio at 2420 Dowling Street in 1925, and Mrs. Teal, who had earned her own reputation, operated the studio on Milam.

Lucille B. Moore worked with Mr. Teal as an assistant from 1925 to 1946, when she left to teach school. Moore took over for Teal when he left to photograph black colleges and schools around the state, including Wiley, Bishop, and

Prairie View.[22] At the colleges, Teal often hired students to advertise his services and set up appointments in advance of his arrival. Ivery Myers, who worked for Teal at Prairie View, says that he was able to pay for his education with the commissions that he earned. After graduation, Myers went on to manage the studio Teal established in San Antonio during World War II.[23]

In 1942 Teal started his own school for photography which he operated independently at his studio. To his students and to the African American community at large, he was renowned as much for his capability as a businessman and entrepreneur as for his craftsmanship and artistry as a photographer.

In an African American community newspaper, the Houston *Informer,* a 1942 article entitled "Teal Studio Steps Out" proudly announced his first graduating class:

> Last Friday night, the Teal Studio, photographers for this sheet, came through with its first graduating class in

Charles G. Harris, *A Few Harris County Survivors of Ante-Bellum Days, Red Book of Houston,* 1915. *Courtesy Metropolitan Research Center, Houston Public Library.*

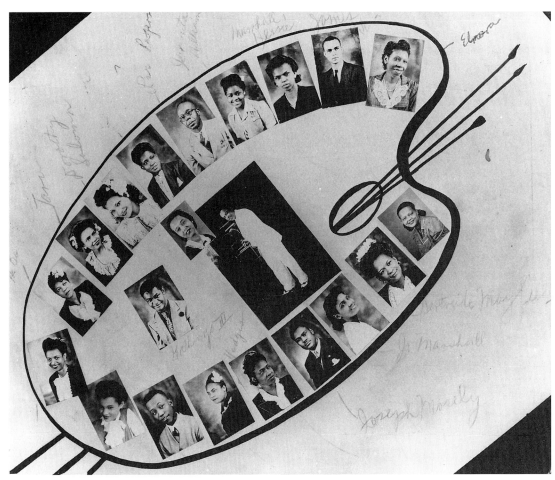

Unknown maker, American school, *Teal School of Photography,* Houston, Texas, 1942.

photography, at the Emancipation clubhouse. The affair was in the form of a banquet, and pretty girl graduates, like pictures, and handsome young esquires made up the class.

Among the graduates were Rosetta Alle, Jesse Brooks, Jennie Crawford, Eva Darrett, Joseph Garner, Tyler Hodges, Willie Manos, George Marsha, Gertrude Mayfield, Joseph Mosely, Catherine Palmer, L. K. Rodgers, Dorothy Solomon, Edna Tarver, James Varner, Elnora Williams, Selina Williams, and Tabertha Williams. Music was furnished by Will Henry Bennett and his bevy of dames from Prairie View college. . . . need I say more about the music. Mr. and Mrs. A C Teal and Joseph Gathings compose the faculty of the school. The little invite carried a miniature photo of the graduates and the faculty. Hats off to the Teals for

this class, and they have invaded a field where there is a dire need of workers and plenty of space to work. A capacity house greeted these youngsters.[24]

Among the graduates of the Teal School of Photography, Benny Joseph, Elnora (Williams) Frazier, and Juanita Williams are represented in this book. According to Elnora Frazier, who worked for Teal from 1942 until his death in 1956, "After Mr. Teal passed away, his wife continued to work as a photographer into the 1960s. Many of the Teal graduates went into photo processing and then on to other jobs. Few opened studios."[25]

Hiram Dotson, originally from Brenham, Texas, attended the Teal School in 1946–1947, and then went to work as a photographer for the Houston *Informer.* After thirteen years with the *Informer,* Dotson became the staff photographer for the *Forward Times* when it was founded by

Julius Carter in 1960. Carter had sold advertising for Carter Wesley at the *Informer*, but left in the mid-1950s to work in the vending business with the intent of eventually starting his own newspaper. Carter died on January 18, 1972, and his wife Lenora Carter assumed the role of publisher, a position she still holds today. However, her daughter Karen Carter worked as the associate publisher and was more involved with the daily operations of the paper. Dotson is now head of the photographic and lithography department.[26]

Teal reportedly operated his school as an adjunct program for the Houston Colored Junior College (started in 1927) and the Houston College for Negroes (founded in 1885), both of which held classes in Jack Yates High School in the Third Ward. In 1946, the Houston College for Negroes moved to a location southeast of downtown Houston on fifty-three acres of land donated by Hugh Roy Cullen, which one year later became the site of the Texas State College for Negroes, which was later renamed Texas Southern University (TSU).

According to historian Cary Wintz,

> The impetus for the acquisition of Houston College for Negroes by the state was the law suit filed by Heman Sweatt in an effort to desegregate the law school at the University of Texas. The Sweatt challenge grew out of a decision of the Texas State Conference of the NAACP in 1945 to target segregation in higher education. When it became clear that Sweatt had a good chance to win his case because the State of Texas had not provided a law school or a full service university for blacks, the legislature attempted to perpetuate the dual system of education by forming a law school and a university for blacks.[27]

The earliest photography instructors at TSU were Edna Tarver, a graduate of Teal's School, and Cliff Richardson, who started teaching in 1947 but left to work for *Sepia* magazine in Fort Worth in 1952. Richardson was replaced by Rodney Evans, who taught at TSU until 1991. Photography at TSU was part of the School of Vocational and Industrial Education with the objective to "provide basic training necessary

for effective employment in trade and industrial pursuits as skilled craftsmen, owners or managers and teachers."[28] Over the years Evans had numerous students who pursued careers in commercial photography. Earlie Hudnall, however, combined his curriculum in photography with his interests in fine arts.

Hudnall acknowledges the importance of Evans as a teacher, but also credits his classmate Ray Carrington, artist John Biggers (also a professor at TSU), and photographer Herbert Provost as influences in his development. Although Hudnall is now recognized as an "art" photographer, he also identifies himself as a

A. C. Teal Funeral Brochure, November 17, 1956, Houston, Texas.

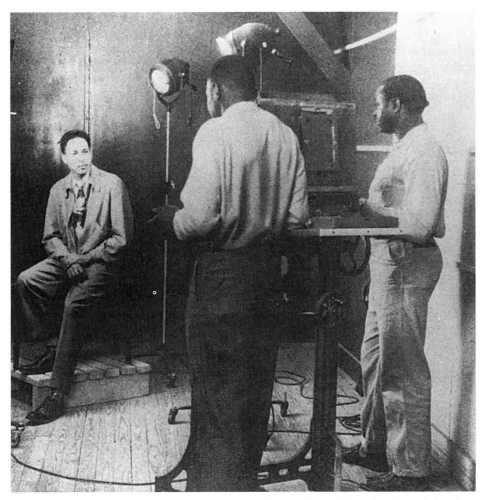

Unknown maker, American school, *Photography Class, The Tiger, Texas Southern University,*
Houston, Texas, 1950.

kind of community photographer. He works at
TSU and devotes much of his time to photographing campus life, as well as neighborhood people and activities.

The degree of training of other African
American photographers in Houston and elsewhere around the state varies. Herbert Provost
and R. C. Hickman learned about photography
in the military and after their discharges from
the service continued to work as photographers. Hickman attended the Southwest School
of Photography in Dallas (certified under the
G.I. Bill of Rights), directed by Roy A. Lay, who
also operated the Southwest School of Mortuary
Science at the same location at 3001 Commerce
Street.[29] Other than Hickman's reminiscences
and an advertisement in the 1947–1948 *Negro
City Directory,* little is known about the
Southwest School of Photography or its proprietor, who was reportedly a photographer him-

self.[30] The most prominent black photogra-
phers in Dallas at that time were Cato Brown,
who worked at 2306 Hall; Reverend Walter
Solomon, at 2212 Hall; M. S. Dunlavy, at 3619
Havana; Marion Butts, at 3504 Munger; Taft
Wilson, at 3408 San Jacinto; Emma King
Woodard, at 3415 Howell; and Dewitt
Humphrey, at 2715 Bryan.[31]

Marion Butts worked for white photographers and learned by watching, as did Calvin
Littlejohn in Fort Worth and Curtis Humphrey
in Tyler. Curtis Humphrey, however, started
his career in Fort Worth, moved to Dallas, and
eventually settled in Tyler. While in Fort
Worth, Curtis Humphrey encouraged his
brother Dewitt to join him and taught him to
be a photographer as well. Dewitt Humphrey
operated his own studio in Dallas until his
death in 1980, when his associate Joseph
Stewart assumed full responsibility.[32]

Louise Martin studied art at Denver University and the Chicago Art Institute.[33] Rodney Evans learned photography at Southern University in Baton Rouge, Louisiana, and later moved to Houston. Elizabeth "Tex" Williams worked as an assistant at the Stanley Reddick Art Studio in Houston, and then bought a Kodak camera to photograph her friends. In 1944 she joined the Women's Army Corps and became an official army photographer. Williams was sent to the Fort Monmouth (New Jersey) Photo Division School in 1949 and continued to work as an army photographer until her retirement in 1970.[34]

In Austin, the community photographers were essentially self-taught and also worked in photography on a part-time basis. Robert L. Whitby was born in Beeville, Texas, in 1914 and moved to Austin in 1935. As a young man, he bought a Kodak Brownie camera to make personal photographs. He attended Tillotson College and graduated in 1941 with a degree in Spanish and a minor in English. After graduation, he was drafted into the army and served in

George Meister, *Marion Butts at Work in the Adolphus Hotel, 1941,* Dallas, Texas.

Unknown maker, American school, *Robert Whitby in the Army,* ca. 1942–1944.

Germany, France, and North Africa during World War II. In 1945 he was discharged and started teaching at Tillotson College. A year later he met Arah Pool, who was originally from Davilla, Texas, and went to Austin to study at Tillotson, where she received a degree in home economics.

They married in 1947, and in 1948 left Austin for Madison, Wisconsin. Mr. Whitby enrolled at the University of Wisconsin and received a Master of Arts degree in Spanish and foreign languages. The Whitbys then moved to Charlotte, North Carolina, where Robert taught at Johnson C. Smith University during the school year 1949–1950, but then returned to Austin to teach at Tillotson College.

Whitby started developing his own negatives in the kitchen of his apartment as early as 1946, and after moving back to Austin he was able to use an enlarger on the Tillotson campus. Eventually he built his own darkroom in a garage storeroom at his house, and in 1950 he bought a Leica camera, which he used throughout his career.

Mrs. Whitby recalls that her husband "made

himself available to the black community in Austin. There were no other black photographers, other than Robert Ross, who had a studio on East 11th Street in the 1930s, but had apparently died or moved away." Although Mr. Whitby was not a professional photographer per se, he did take photographs for schools, special events, and conventions. He also did considerable work for African American sororities and fraternities, including Delta Sigma Theta, Zeta Phi Beta, and Alpha Kappa, as well as for churches, such as the Simpson Methodist Church, Wesley United Methodist Church, David Chapel, and Rising Star Church.

While Mr. Whitby worked at Tillotson, Mrs. Whitby got a job teaching special education in the Austin Independent School District. In 1952 Tillotson College merged with Sam Huston College to become Huston-Tillotson, and in 1956 Robert accepted a position at Anderson High School, where he taught Spanish and foreign languages until 1965. He then returned to Huston-Tillotson and worked there until his retirement in 1977.[35]

During Whitby's tenure at Anderson High

School, he met Morris Crawford, who also had a personal interest in photography and who took over much of Whitby's part-time work after his death. In the book is an oral history by Crawford's son, who provides details about his father's life and career.

Although Whitby and Crawford were able to meet most of the needs of people in their community, many went to the white-owned studios for formal portraits. Aside from their limited capability as portrait photographers, Whitby and Crawford worked in their community in much the same manner as their contemporaries around the state. Their personal photographs, however, were basically vernacular in nature and were similar to the kinds of snapshots taken today by numerous people in their communities. What made Whitby's and Crawford's work more desirable at that time was the relative sophistication of their equipment, including Leica and Speed Graphic cameras, and their knowledge of darkroom techniques.

The extent to which African American vernacular and community photography in Texas differs from that of other culturally specific photographers is difficult to assess. Certainly, given the social, political, and economic obstacles imposed by segregation and discrimination, African Americans developed a cultural and aesthetic sensibility apart from the mainstream.

While most early black photographers operated studios outside the central business areas and thus lessened the possibility of white crossover patronage, Curtis Humphrey, Marion Butts, Benny Joseph, and Robert Whitby did have occasional white clients. This crossover patronage, however, is not uncommon in the history of African American photography. Jules Lion and J. P. Ball, for example, were among the first African American daguerreotypists and made their living from both white and black subjects. Moreover, the Goodridge Brothers (ca. 1841–1922), Harry Shepherd (ca. 1887–1904), and Gordon Parks (b. 1912) photographed people of different nationalities and ethnicities.[36]

What distinguishes the work of African American photographers in general is their emphasis upon document and social record. Consequently, art historian Deborah Johnson suggests, "It is perhaps a more direct and effective barometer of the social and economic history of a people than can usually be expected from an art form. It is also, to an unusual extent, a result of that history. This is not to say that it is all naive or 'artless.'"[37]

Certainly one of the primary goals of the African American photographers in Texas was to show their subjects at their best. Community photographers have had an essential role in the day-to-day lives of the people they serve. In addition to documenting events and activities, they reinforce community values and self-esteem. Art historian Alvia Wardlaw, who grew up in the African American community of Houston, asserts that "During the era of the 1940s and '50s, when black photographers were making their living as independent businessmen, there was a need in the community to project a very positive image of themselves. These [photographs] were not found in the larger publications. They were published in the Houston *Informer* and the *Forward Times*. The photographs were essential vehicles for maintaining a positive sense of self. There was a formality that was required in presenting the very polished image the photographers were able to provide to people. Physical dignity was very important during the period of segregation. It was like a counter-action. There's a vibrancy and pride that is apparent in the photographic portraits."[38]

All of the photographers in this book acknowledge this function of their work for their subjects. Carl Sidle and Earlie Hudnall, however, have a somewhat different approach than most of the others. While they still concern themselves with the presentation of community life, they initiate their photography at their own expense. In part, their photographs draw attention to the decay of the community. Yet their focus is life-affirming and emphasizes what they consider to be the dignity of their subjects despite adversity.

Sidle, in his photographs of people peering around doors and through half-open windows, is concerned with the fears and anxieties of life in the inner city. He also prints negatives on top of each other to accentuate the psychological tension and, perhaps, the spiritual union between people and the places they inhabit. This technique creates a photomontage effect, and is similar to the "combination printing" practiced by photographers in the late nineteenth century, as well as by noted Harlem photographer James Van Der Zee during the 1920s and 1930s.[39] It is also a technique used in the mass media.

Hudnall, on the other hand, visualizes the sometimes contradictory and ironic beauty of community life: homeless people on public benches, persons dressed-up in run-down Fourth Ward neighborhoods, children playing in front of dilapidated shotgun houses with the impersonal postmodern Houston skyline looming behind them. In his photographs, Hudnall expresses compassion for and understanding of his subjects. Through his prints, ordinary people are imbued with importance. In this way, Hudnall acknowledges his link to the community photographers who preceded him. Ultimately, he strives to depict the quality of life, rather than simply documenting the conditions of poverty. His subjects may lack the trappings of prosperity, but they nevertheless display dignity and vitality.

African American photographers have historically had an aesthetic imperative. A. C. Teal, for example, advertised that he made "Photography of a Better Kind." The aesthetics of the finished print, however, were shaped largely by the desires and needs of his subjects. Teal was recognized for his ability to retouch negatives, although, given the vastness of his clientele, he often employed others to utilize his techniques in the actual process. Nonetheless, through retouching negatives and hand-tinting prints, the Teal Studio removed blemishes and altered skin tones to create idealized portraits. Similarly, Curtis Humphrey, Calvin Littlejohn, Benny Joseph, and the others experimented with retouching and different printing methods, including diffusing filters, dodging, and burning to yield highlights and special effects.

Community photographers also used a variety of lighting techniques, though not always to their customers' satisfaction. Benny Joseph recalled using Rembrandt lighting, but his subjects often complained that "one side of their face was too dark."[40] Elnora Frazier, however, successfully used dramatic lighting to highlight faces or gestures, and sometimes tinted her prints with exaggerated coloration. Louise Martin occasionally used softer lighting to achieve a more expressive quality, especially evident in her portrait of Coretta Scott King.

To varying degrees, community photographers were influenced by "pictorialism" and the "glamour style" with its soft focus and artificial lighting that eliminated the background and had a shallow depth of field to isolate the subjects' faces or eyes. This approach was used by numerous black photographers around the country, including Addison N. Scurlock in Washington, D.C., and P. H. Polk at the Tuskegee Institute in Alabama.[41]

Earlie Hudnall generally uses natural lighting and focuses on the formal properties of composition as it appears in the context of the everyday world on the street. For example, in his "Lady in Plaid Skirt," the viewer sees only the back of someone who appears to be an old woman and the spread of her youthful skirt. The spatial relationship between form and line may be dominant, but the underlying psychology of the situation is impossible to ignore. Who is this woman, and why is she wearing these clothes in this place at this particular time?

While Hudnall and Sidle do interact with their subjects, the nature of that interaction is significantly different than that of the other community photographers. About this interaction, Wardlaw suggests "there is often a sense of human drama and the humor that is so present in the black community in terms of exchanges. When you look at the photographs, you want to comment. There's going to be an exchange, a recognition. They're capturing the repartee that you hear."

The camera is always an outsider, but the photographer mediates the distance from the subject. If the photographer is of the same culture, then that becomes a mediating influence. But the camera is still outside the inner frame of what's really happening. To be able to photograph a culture, one has to understand the values that are present. The quintessential moment is where experience comes together in a way that is reflective of not only the situation that you're seeing, but of the world of which it is a part. Perhaps, the most difficult aspect of culture to photograph is humor because humor is culturally specific.[42]

Hudnall and Sidle determine the composition and printing style of their images themselves and are not restricted by the approval or disapproval of their subjects. Generally, community photographers depend on the acceptance of their work for their livelihood, and consequently the interaction between them and their subjects is necessarily more direct.

In some respects, discussion of the aesthetics of these community photographers is external to their own perception of their work. About the significance of photography in African American community life, Wardlaw comments,

> There was a conservative attitude when it came to photography. The informational value was its primary significance. People didn't have many photographs made, especially prior to World War II. The photographic event was considered an important occasion, but the power of the individual photograph was greater. The photographer was perceived as a functionary kind of person, and once the photograph went beyond the identifiable purpose, then it was questioned.[43]

Most of the photographers had little direct interest in art. Marion Butts, Benny Joseph, and Herbert Provost say that they were too busy making a living to think about art. Louise Martin, however, always considered herself an artist, although most of her work was commercial. Martin was more demanding and selective than many of her contemporaries. Her aesthetic standards were implicit in her choice of composition and control over tonal values. During her heyday from the late 1940s through the 1970s, Martin was considered a "society" photographer who specialized in hand-tinting and oil coloring. In 1973, she founded the Louise Martin School of Photography and offered courses in all branches of black-and-white photography. Her complete photo course involved sixteen weeks of training, two hours a day, four days a week. In addition, she offered separate courses in fundamental photography, advanced techniques, flash photography, advanced portraiture, commercial and industrial techniques, and photo oil coloring. Unfortunately, she was forced to close her school in 1976 because of financial problems.

Elnora Frazier, who worked for Teal and then for commercial photo processing and printing companies, did her own personal photography at home. These images featured family and friends, and together, they constitute her most accomplished work. About these photographs she says, "I put the most energy into the photographs of my family and friends. I worked hard at the printing and used fiber papers. I did hand-tinting, and I did not tint for anyone else."[44] Although these photographs are essentially vernacular in nature, they were made with an aesthetic intent. They may have been functional in that they provided records of family events, but they were nonetheless artistic.

Curtis Humphrey admits that he wanted to be an artist when he was a child, but had to find ways to support himself through a variety of jobs. With photography, he says, he could be more creative, but rarely had the opportunity to pursue his personal interests. Carl Sidle and Earlie Hudnall have jobs as professional photographers, and engage in their personal work in their free time.

To distinguish between those photographs that are "art" and those that are not is beyond the scope of this book. The relative significance of functional and art photography remains open to interpretation and debate. John Szarkowski, former curator of photography at the Museum of Modern Art, suggests that snapshots and vernacular prints can be the aesthetic peers of "fine art" photographs.[45] Pepe Karmel, in reviewing the *Century of Black Photographers* exhibition, concludes: "On the one hand, political exigencies can overpower the imperatives of art; on the other, the desire to be accepted as an artist can lead the black photographer to betray his own experience. It is a painful dilemma, but it offers an opportunity: to use the 'raised consciousness' of politics to alter and enrich the received language of art."[46]

The aesthetics of the photographs presented here may vary in sophistication and political intent, but together they are a powerful portrait of African American family and community life in Texas. They form an undeniable link to the past and enhance our understanding of the contemporary world. John Berger suggests that

> Photographs are relics of the past, traces of what has happened. If the living take that past upon themselves, if the past becomes an integral part of the process of people making their own history, then all photographs would reacquire a living context, they would continue to exist in time, instead of being arrested moments. It is just possible that photography is the prophecy of a human memory yet to be achieved. Such a memory would encompass any image of the past, however tragic, however guilty, within its own community.[47]

The work of these photographers shows a remarkable continuity and a deep regional influence that overshadows the wide variations in their training and careers. This book is comprehensive in scope, but not definitive. Implicit is the assumption that further study is needed of these photographers and of vernacular and community photography in general. In sum, the book examines African American life in Texas over the last century and places the work of older photographers alongside that of their younger peers from around the state. In the book Texas serves a metonymic purpose, offering a forum for the reassessment of history in the broader context of African American experience and its representation.

NOTES

1. Richard Pearce-Moses, *Historic Texas: A Photographic Portrait* (Austin: Texas Monthly Press, 1986).

2. Beaumont Newhall, *The History of Photography* (New York: Museum of Modern Art, 1982).

3. Valencia Hollins Coar, *A Century of Black Photographers, 1840–1960* (Providence: Rhode Island School of Design, 1983).

4. Nicholas Natanson, *The Black Image in the New Deal: The Politics of FSA Photography* (Knoxville: University of Tennessee Press, 1992).

5. Alan Govenar, *Living Texas Blues* (Dallas: Dallas Museum of Art, 1985). See also Rick Stewart, *Lone Star Regionalism: The Dallas Nine and Their Circle* (Austin: Texas Monthly Press, 1985).

6. James Cone, *A Black Theology of Liberation* (New York: Orbis, 1990).

7. Interview with Teresa Sidle Hardeman, Feb. 1, 1993. For more information on tintypes and other early photographic processes, see William Crawford, *A History and Working Guide to Early Photographic Processes* (Dobbs Ferry: Morgan and Morgan, 1979), and Floyd and Marion Rinhart, *The American Daguerreotype* (Athens: University of Georgia Press, 1981).

8. David Haynes, *Catching Shadows: A Directory of Nineteenth-Century Texas Photographers* (Austin: Texas State Historical Association, 1993), 3, 6, 13, 17, 20–21, 32, 49, 66, 98, 108.

9. *Hidden Witness: African Americans in Early Photography*, J. Paul Getty Museum, Feb. 28–June 18, 1995.

10. For more information on Underwood and Underwood and Keystone stereographs, see William Culp Darrah, *Stereoviews: A History of Stereographs in America and Their Collection* (Gettysburg, Pa.: Darrah, 1964), 109–116, and Edward W. Earle (ed.), *Point of View: The Stereograph in America, A Cultural History* (Rochester: Visual Studies Workshop Press, 1979).

11. Quoted in Michael R. Winston, "Historical Consciousness and the Photographic Moment," in Coar, *A Century of Black Photographers*, 23. For more information, see Rayford W. Logan, *The Negro in the United States* (New York: Van Nostrand Reinhold, 1957), and Rayford W. Logan, *The American Negro* (New York: Houghton Mifflin, 1970).

12. Winston, "Historical Consciousness and the Photographic Moment," 23.

13. Dannehl Twomey, "Into the Mainstream: Early Black Photography in Houston," *Houston Review*, IX, No. 1 (1987), 39–48.

14. Haynes, *Catching Shadows*, 6, 10, 24, 95, 110, 111.

15. Angela Davis, "Photography and Afro-American History," in Coar, *A Century of Black Photographers*, 25 (quotation), 27.

16. John D. Weaver, *The Brownsville Raid* (New York: W. W. Norton, 1970); Ann J. Lane, *The Brownsville Affair: Crisis and Black Reaction* (Port Washington: Kennikat Press, 1971); *The Crisis* (New York: National Association for the Advancement of Colored People), XIII (Feb. 1917).

17. Description on back of stereograph (CN 01049), Prints and Photographs Collection, Blacks file, Center for American History, University of Texas at Austin (cited hereafter as CAH) (1st quotation); description on back of print (CN 02873), ibid. (2nd quotation); Kansas City *Star*, Feb. 2, 1893, clipping in Prints and Photographs

Collection, Paris, Texas, file (CAH) (3rd quotation); CN 03113, CN 03114, Roy Wilkinson Aldrich Papers, 1858–1955 (CAH).

18. Twomey, "Into the Mainstream," 39.

19. Ibid., 41. See also Richard Pearce-Moses, *Photographic Collections in Texas: A Union Code* (College Station: Texas A&M University Press, 1987).

20. *The Red Book of Houston* (Houston: Sotex, 1915).

21. Telephone interview with Patricia Smith Prather, Houston Place Preservation Association, Dec. 9, 1993.

22. For more information on Elnora Teal, see Jeanne Moutoussomy-Ashe, *Viewfinders: Black Women Photographers* (New York: Dodd, Mead and Co., 1985), 44–45.

23. Interview with Ivery Myers, Oct. 13, 1993.

24. Houston *Informer*, 1942, undated clipping from Elnora Frazier.

25. Interview with Elnora Frazier, Mar. 16, 1993.

26. Telephone interview with Hiram Dotson, Dec. 10, 1993. For more information on Carter Wesley, see Nancy Echols Bessent, "The Publisher: A Biography of Carter Wesley" (M.A. thesis, University of Texas at Austin, 1981), and Charles W. Grose, "Black Newspapers in Texas" (Ph.D. diss., University of Texas at Austin, 1973).

27. Cary Wintz, "Texas Southern University," in Ron Tyler, Doug Barnett, and Roy Barkley (eds.), *New Handbook of Texas* (6 vols.; Austin: Texas State Historical Association, forthcoming 1996). See also Alwyn Barr and Robert A. Calvert, *Black Leaders: Texans for Their Times* (Austin: Texas State Historical Association, 1981).

28. *The 1952 Tiger* (Houston: Texas Southern University, 1952).

29. For more information on R. C. Hickman, see the R. C. Hickman Collection at the Center for American History, University of Texas at Austin. See also R. C. Hickman, *Behold the People: R.C. Hickman's Photographs of Black Dallas, 1949–1961* (Austin: Texas State Historical Association, 1994).

30. Interview with Bernice Humphrey, Dec. 15, 1993.

31. *Dallas, Texas, Negro City Directory, 1947–1948* (Dallas: Dallas Times Herald, 1947).

32. Interview with Curtis Humphrey, Sept. 26, 1993.

33. For more information on Louise Martin, see Moutoussomy-Ashe, *Viewfinders*, 87–91.

34. For more information on Elizabeth "Tex" Williams, see ibid., 98–100.

35. Interview with Arah Whitby, Feb. 1, 1993.

36. Coar, *A Century of Black Photographers*, 9–12. See also Deborah Willis-Thomas, *Black Photographers, 1840–1940: An Illustrated Bio-Bibliography* (New York: Garland Publishing, 1985); Deborah Willis-Thomas (ed.), *J. P. Ball: Daguerrean and Studio Photographer* (New York, Garland Publishing, 1993); and Gordon Parks, *Gordon Parks: A Poet and His Camera* (London: Deutsch, 1969).

37. Deborah J. Johnson, "Black Photography: Contexts for Evolution," in Coar, *A Century of Black Photographers*, 17.

38. Interview with Alvia Wardlaw, Oct. 16, 1988.

39. Deborah Willis-Braithwaite, *Van Der Zee: Photographer, 1886–1983* (New York: Harry N. Abrams, 1993), 16–17.

40. Interview with Benny Joseph, July 22, 1989. See also Alan Govenar, *The Early Years of Rhythm and Blues* (Houston: Rice University Press, 1991), 14–20.

41. For more information, see Joe Brown, "Washington Kaleidoscope," Washington *Post*, July 19, 1991 (review of the exhibition *African American Photography in Washington, D.C.*, at the Anacostia Museum); Gene Thornton, "P. H. Polk's Genius vs. Modernism," New York *Times*, Feb. 21, 1982; Jane Livingston, *P. H. Polk* (Washington: Corcoran Gallery of Art, 1981).

42. Interview with Alvia Wardlaw, Oct. 16, 1988.

43. Ibid.

44. Interview with Elnora Frazier, Mar. 16, 1993.

45. John Szarkowski, *The Photographer's Eye* (New York: Museum of Modern Art, 1966).

46. Pepe Karmel, "Photography Terra Incognita," in *Art in America*, LXXI (Oct. 1983), 42–43.

47. John Berger, *About Looking* (New York: Pantheon, 1980), 57. For more detailed information about the importance of photography in the study of history and culture, see "Taylor Made Pictures," Center for Southern Folklore, Memphis, Tennessee, 1980 (brochure); Frederic M. Miller, Morris J. Vogel, and Allen F. Davis (eds.), *A Photographic History* (Philadelphia: Temple University Press, 1983); and Elizabeth Edwards (ed.), *Anthropology and Photography, 1860–1920* (New Haven: Yale University Press, 1992).

Teresa Sidle Hardeman

My father was a horse trader who moved from Pflugerville to Austin after I was born on May 27, 1918. His name was Simon Sidle. And he'd go around in his truck and find so many antiques he started a business for himself. He would sell them on Red River, at Red River and Tenth Street in Austin. He worked in a big old two story building, and I used to carry him lunch. So, I fell in love with antiques, and I used to go out with him looking for them. We went out to the country people and we'd go and buy antiques from them. We would go into the basements, but he never would approach them directly. He would always talk about the farm first and then they'd let him go down in the basement. He'd buy some of the most beautiful china and pretty trunks and old furniture. A lot of it was painted because they tried to modernize it, but it was old and we would do the stripping. There were twelve of us children, but only three boys. One of the boys went to the shop with him and he tried to teach him, but he never did take it up. I was the only one out of the twelve that was interested. And later on in 1962 my sister Alesta got handicapped and she got interested. She was in a wreck and lost one of her legs. So, she went into the business and started Johnny's Antiques.

I'm a historian-gatherer. I have old books and old photographs. I've got a little collection of everything pertaining to history. Some of it I got from my father, like some of the tintypes he got from the people around here. I'm sure some came from old albums and old houses I used to go in. I'd get in and pick all that up. They cared nothing about them in those days.

I did a lot of reading and research when I would have nothing to do after I first opened my place at 1122 Red River. I just worked to build up my trade and everything. I had people coming from all over the United States to visit my place because I had something for everybody. I'm sure that the tintypes came from homes here, but I don't know all the people because a lot of them were before my time.

I used to work for a Mrs. Steven here. She was an old lady then and I was about eleven years of age. Her son had a studio on Congress Avenue. His name was Mr. Boone. He was a white photographer who took a lot of pictures of black people. We didn't have many photographers. That was before my time.

I cleaned the kitchen for his mother. I cut her toenails and things like that, combed her hair, played with her. She was my baby. I always loved old folks a lot. I was a kid at that time, and I don't know exactly what her son did. There were other photographers on Congress Avenue.

In those days everybody didn't have a camera like they have now, and black people weren't able. We had school pictures, like when I graduated. That was a luxury to have a little Kodak. I don't think many black people even had cameras that I can remember. I know we didn't have one in our family. And my daddy was accessible to a lot of things but he never did bring us nothing but toys. We got those at Christmas. I can remember we played with our dolls. I remember we had things that we were knowledgeable about, like church; we'd have a choir and we'd have films and we'd have solo singing. We'd play with our dolls, and we'd always go down on East Avenue to a big old mesquite tree and just play, play, play. And there was a big lot next to our place, and a lot of times we'd sit there watching those wagons that went up on to Fort Worth to sell their cattle. They would pass by.

My father's family lived in Brenham. His mother was named Mary Sidle. There were white Sidles there. She was formerly from Tennessee. My father's mother came from slavery and that's the name they took from the white family. My grandmother was 103 when she passed. She was a baby born right when slavery was abolished.

Unknown maker, American school, *Seated Couple*, Austin, Texas (?), ca. 1880. *Teresa Sidle Hardeman Collection.*

Unknown maker, American school, *Standing Boy*, Austin, Texas (?), ca. 1870–1880. *Teresa Sidle Hardeman Collection.*

Unknown maker, *Couple*, Austin, Texas (?), ca. 1880–1890. *Teresa Sidle Hardeman Collection.*

Morris Crawford Jr.

My father took photographs at community functions at the St. James Baptist Church right next door, the Olivet Baptist Church, the Wesley Methodist Church, and I'm sure when I was a child he took some at the Holy Cross Church and most of the other black churches in Austin. Then he photographed graduation ceremonies at the black colleges, commencements at the high schools, and Christmas plays at the elementary schools. He went out to the sororities and fraternities, debutante balls, and most of the activities at Huston-Tillotson College.

I got interested in photography after my father passed. I came home and took a few courses at the University of Texas myself, refresher courses. I was born on November 5, 1947, and my sister, Karen, was born a year later on September 27, 1948. My father really taught me the main functions of photography, black-and-white photography at any rate. He always had a camera with him when we were kids. And I took some courses in color photography, and I want to continue where he left off. I work as an independent operator. I drive a Ford LTL9000, conventional tractor rig. Not many other folks in my family really got into photography on the professional level, because my father could handle anything that came up himself.

My father did work for the NAACP and for other political functions. He took pictures of Congresswoman Wilhemina Delco back in her early years. He used to go over to the Graham Lodge over on Eleventh Street and the Masonic Temple for their fairs and special events.

My father died December 30, 1983, when he was sixty-three years old. He was born November 30, 1920, in Texarkana. He went to Prairie View from Texarkana, and that's where he met my mom and they moved back here to

Austin, where she was from. He was in the Coast Guard during the war. My mother's maiden name was Lucille Kathryn Dotson, and she had grown up in Austin. She had family here.

Going through some of these pictures, I'm really remembering why my father got into taking pictures, group pictures, more or less professional pictures. It was because of my mother. My mother was the physical education director at Anderson High School, and she was in charge of the cheerleaders, the pep squad, and all the girls in the school. And she made my father come take pictures of her Capezio Clubs and the cheerleaders and the National Honor Society and her committee groups because they were a thing of beauty to see—all her black and gold girls on the fields, twirling and carrying on. My father had to take those group pictures. As I remember, my father was really a busy person in my high school days. He was a referee, an umpire, around the state and counties. He refereed football games, and I remember my mother having her special halftime shows. He might have to go referee a game in some distant county, and my mother told him, "No, you can't go referee. You have to stay and take these pictures tonight of my girls on the field." And he'd take snapshots and photographs of uncontrolled situations and they were great, but his studio shots were really things of beauty. They were really representative of the caliber of photography he took.

There were debutante activities once or twice a year, given by the different sororities and the service fraternities. They would come right here to the house and he would have his backdrop paper or sheets or screens and special trick lenses. There would be a real assembly line with the number of girls in the house. They filled all the bedrooms and came through in line. The girls were chattering and being nervous, and he tried to make them feel at home and at ease to get the best pose and get their personality to really show up on the paper.

In the 1950s and early '60s, my father was a vocational agriculture teacher at Anderson High School. That's when he met Mr. Robert Whitby, who taught Spanish and French at Anderson High and was also a photographer. Mr. Whitby influenced my father a lot, and when Mr. Whitby got sick, my father kind of took over. He got a Speed Graphic camera and two Nikons. He started taking photographs by request and before long people would come knocking at his door. He built his own dark-room in the mid-1960s. I graduated Anderson High in 1965, and in 1971 Anderson High closed and my dad went to Burnet Junior High School, where he was vice-principal until he died. He got cancer of the lymph nodes, and on the day he died he was supposed to take pictures.

Robert Whitby, *Morris Crawford*, Austin, Texas, ca. 1950s.

Morris Crawford, *L. C. Anderson High School Choir*, Austin, Texas, ca. 1965.

Morris Crawford, *Capezio Club*, Austin, Texas, ca. 1957–1958.

Morris Crawford, *Lucille Crawford*, Austin, Texas, ca. 1983.

Morris Crawford, *Robert Whitby, The Yellow Jacket, Anderson High School Yearbook,* Austin, Texas, 1963.

Robert Whitby, *Children with Hula Hoops,* Austin, Texas, ca. 1957.

Robert Whitby, *Felicia and Arah Whitby,* Austin, Texas, ca. 1951.

Robert Whitby, *East Austin*, Texas, ca. 1950s.

Robert Whitby, *Music School Graduation*, Austin, Texas, ca. 1950s.

Robert Whitby, *Crowning of Miss Huston-Tillotson*, Austin, Texas, 1954–1955.

Robert Whitby, *Arah Whitby and Viola Williams, Groundbreaking, Bethany Christian Church*, Austin, Texas, 1965.

Marion Butts

I grew up in Burleson County in a little place in the country called Tunis, nine miles east of Caldwell, Texas, where I was born on April 26, 1924. In the country we celebrated Juneteenth, and whites celebrated the Fourth of July, and we didn't for some reason, I don't know why. On Juneteenth there was lemonade, barbecue, and maybe some blues, but none of the famous blues singers came through where I lived.

I came to Dallas in December 1941. My mother and two sisters were living in Dallas at the time I moved here. I was living in Bryan, and I don't really remember what brought me. I came to be with the rest of the family.

I had an uncle working at the Adolphus Hotel and I needed a job. He knew two photographers, George Meister and Morris Landolph, who were doing business at the hotel. I think they were both Jewish. They were good people, especially Meister. He took an interest in me as a young man. He was just like another black man to me and he took an interest in me and really was almost like a father. They had the concession all over the hotel and also at the Century Room. They would do photographs in the Century Room while parties were going on. They had their darkroom on the twentieth floor and they needed somebody to bring the film to the darkroom for processing and deliver the photographs back to the Century Room. That's how I got the job, and I was making one dollar per night, and on Saturdays I used to work maybe four or five hours and I'd get an extra dollar. Also, I would sometimes get a tip of a dollar.

Well, he asked me if I would be interested in learning how to process the photographs in the darkroom. So I told him "Yes," and he pulled me off the elevator and put me in the dark-room, and in twelve weeks' time I had mastered the darkroom techniques. Then he left, went to the service, and I ran the darkroom, until I had to go to the service. Then I pulled the other young man off that we had put on the elevator and put him in the darkroom.

I was in the navy and went to New Guinea and the Philippines. I missed the opportunity to go to Pensacola, Florida, to the Naval Photographic School. In boot camp, if you get sick, you lose your original company. I had the mumps and they put me in the hospital for two months. When I came out, I had to get in another company, and missed the opportunity to go to school. The navy was totally segregated at the time. The black units stayed and ate together.

While I was in the navy, my mother threw away a lot of my photographs. I started photography in 1943 before I went to the service in 1944, and maybe I had five hundred negatives, I really don't remember. I was only able to preserve two photographs: one was a picture I made of Lena Horne and a reporter with the Dallas *Express* weekly newspaper and the other one was a picture of Joe Lewis when he was traveling for the U.S.O. during World War II. The only reason I had those two photographs is that I put them in my album to take overseas so I could have something to brag about. And when I returned, I made negatives from those two prints.

When I returned from the service, there were no jobs for me, but Meister told me his wife had saved $17,000 because of the work that I did and the work that the other young man did in the darkroom while he was in the service. He had no jobs for me. So he offered to sell me some equipment and/or let me use his darkroom until I could purchase some equipment. He sold me some used equipment. He wouldn't sell it to me on credit, but he did take me to Mercantile Bank, where I borrowed $1,000 and paid him off. Then I paid the loan at the bank, and I guess that was a good business experience for me because I can understand now why he didn't serve it to me on credit, because he probably thought I was soft-talking and wouldn't pay.

While I was in the service, Landolph got killed as a pilot of a small airplane. The fact is, he had taken me for an airplane ride in a little two-seater, and if I had to do it now, I wouldn't take that ride, but he flew me all over the city of Dallas.

Well, I bought a Speed Graphic camera and an Elwood enlarger, developing trays, and developing tanks. I opened a small studio in the old North Dallas area across from St. Peter's Catholic school and church, on Cochran and Allen Streets, and I stayed there four or five years. Primarily I did activities at churches, dance halls, weddings, and events. I did do portraits at the studio, but somehow I didn't like having to be confined at the studio, waiting on people to come in for appointments. So most of my work has been community activities.

I remember a photographic studio in the Thomas and Hall Streets area. The photographer's name was Cato Brown, and he concentrated really on portraits. He didn't go out in the community and do any photography to amount to anything. He was there in the 1930s. I have a photograph he made of me. But I really don't know how long he worked in Dallas. He moved to Washington, D.C., probably in the mid-'50s and I haven't heard from him. I've heard of people who had gone to Washington and said he made it there, but I don't know what happened to his collection.

I moved from my studio into the office of the Dallas *Express* at 2604 Thomas in about 1954. And I stopped running the studio because I was working directly for the Dallas *Express,* and I stayed there until 1964. I became the managing editor of the Dallas *Express.* Carter Wesley was the publisher. He was a retired lawyer, and he operated a chain of newspapers. He had the Houston *Informer,* which was published twice weekly; one edition came out on Tuesday and the other one came out on Thursday. Then he had an edition in New Orleans, and also I believe it was in Port Arthur, Beaumont, and

Austin. I think they were all called the *Informer* except for the one in Dallas. He had bought the Dallas *Express* from someone else, and he kept the name until the paper went out of business in about 1966.

Carter Wesley was a courageous man, very courageous. Whatever he thought needed to be written about, he wrote it. And the Texas Rangers beat him up once for writing a story about the Rangers. He headlined that just like he would if somebody else had gotten beat up. I believe that was in the late 1940s.

When I first came to Dallas, I was a country boy and I heard about Deep Ellum, but there's very little history I know about the place. The area around Hall and Thomas had a better reputation. I went to the Rose Room on Hall Street. I used to do photographs of tables and parties at the Rose Room. I photographed special occasions like the ones held by the American Woodman, possibly two or three special dances a year. We had plenty of social clubs at the time. Almost every weekend, some social club would have a dance at the Rose Room. Some of the best musicians played the Rose Room: T Bone Walker, Buster Smith, Ernie Fields, Jimmy Bell, and others.

I met my wife, Florence Keller Butts, in 1946 and we married in 1949. She grew up in North Dallas. Her grandfather was one of the big farmers in North Dallas. He had come from Tennessee probably in the late 1920s. He grew mainly cotton and corn.

I met my wife around old man Clint Murchison's swimming pool. The land on which he had his house had been part of the farm owned by my wife's grandfather. It's in far North Dallas near Plano, and Keller Springs Road was named for my wife's grandfather. Well, my wife's uncle on her mother's side was working for Clint Murchison and he got married around the pool. The way I got invited was through the pastor of my church, who recommended that members of the Junior Usher Board participate in the wedding.

Bishop College opened an extension school in 1946 called Bishop Center in Dallas across the street from Booker T. Washington High School, and I went there for two years. Then I went to the campus in Marshall for two years. While I was a student, I did all of the photography on the campus in Marshall, plus I worked in the business office as a filing clerk for fifteen cents an hour. And after I started working at Bishop on almost a daily basis, I started looking at photography as an art form.

Bishop College moved to Dallas in 1960 and I did very little work for them until 1966, but in 1966 I was on call. I was working with the student publications, the yearbook, the college catalogue, and all publicity photographs.

I did a lot of school photography on special occasions like American Education Week, Law Day, May Day, and all activities: football, basketball. Whatever they did I photographed it. And I photographed Negro Achievement Day at the State Fair.

I used a Speed Graphic until the early '60s and then I switched to a Rolleiflex and the 2¼ format. I also use 35mm cameras, primarily a Pentax, though I've also used a Canon. And I've had Besseler and Omega enlargers.

Over the years, I learned how to analyze every negative mentally and count, but now I have a timer, especially if I'm going to do multiple prints on one negative. I set the timer and I don't do the old-fashioned counting any more. But if I've just got one print to make on one negative, I still count rows and use the timer. My techniques haven't changed.

A. B. Bell was kind of an apprentice to me. He was a native of Tyler, but he was already in Dallas when I moved here. He was taking a course in photography at Sears Roebuck and I was manager of the Dallas *Express*. I needed a circulation person to distribute papers. So I offered him a job as a circulation man and that also gave him an opportunity to take photographic assignments because I couldn't handle it all. With a weekly newspaper, we'd have so many events at the same time.

Dewitt Humphrey was another black photographer who worked in Dallas a long time. He also came from the Tyler area. His brother, Curtis, worked in Tyler. Dewitt Humphrey had a studio in South Dallas.

I've had offices in different locations. I had a studio at Oakland and Carpenter from about 1962 through 1975, and that's when I stopped having a studio. I continued taking photographs and had an office and a darkroom. I moved from Oakland and Carpenter to a location above the Crawford Funeral Home on Good Latimer. They had an upstairs part above the funeral home, which used to house the black chamber of commerce until around the time I moved in. But they had a fire in 1986 and I moved to Forest Avenue, next to the Forest Theatre, above George Keaton's place, and I stayed there about a year, and moved to my current location at 1412 Bonnieview at the corner of Cedar Crest in 1988.

In the '40s, I'd charge $2.50, and extra prints would cost a dollar. And I would ride a bicycle from old North Dallas to South Dallas around Oakland Avenue. I did wallet-sized photographs, 4×5s, 8×10s, 11×14s, 16×20s and once in a while a 20×24. A couple had a wedding anniversary at the Majestic Theater and they wanted two photographs to go on the marquee so that when people came they could see their portraits outside. I think those photographs were an off-size because we had to make it to accommodate that marquee. They were probably 25x32.

Very seldom do I get more than $25 for a black-and-white print, unless it's something special, like Martin Luther King or Sammy Davis. Sammy Davis Jr. once played golf here, with a local businessman named Harvey Barkins. He was in the beauty-supply business.

I photographed Martin Luther King and a local minister, Reverend Rick James, who pastored at that time at the historic New Hope Baptist Church. Also in the picture there were two other people, an insurance man with Atlanta Life and the Jewish rabbi at that time. Later, I photographed Ralph Bunche, who came here for the World Council, and then Lena Horne, Adam Clayton Powell, Thurgood Marshall, Muhammad Ali, and even President Harry Truman. At that time, I was working for the Dallas *Express*. Normally, I didn't go to the airport unless somebody black was involved, but nobody was involved in that but the President, and we did a story on him when he came because he desegregated the armed forces.

I have done one Mexican wedding during my career and I've done one interracial wedding between Mexicans and blacks. And I believe back in the '50s I did a couple, a white and a black, who were students at the University of Texas.

I did a lot of photography for the NAACP. I probably have about 150 negatives I did at the

NAACP convention in Dallas. I believe that was in 1956. So I might have 200 to 300 negatives on the NAACP or more because I did all the local branch work.

I don't think blacks in Dallas really fought like they did in other areas. We benefited from what they did elsewhere, although we did have to do some fighting—like Skillern's Drugs; you could go in and purchase anything you want, but you couldn't get a job. So we had to picket. And there was the Lakeland Theater down in South Dallas, where nobody but black people lived and nobody attended this theater but black people. And they had a black union of motion-picture machine operators and they couldn't get jobs there. So they had to picket to get jobs.

At the Majestic Theater they had what we called the Crow's Nest where you had to go upstairs and you had a separate entrance and everything. And I believe that was the only theater downtown that blacks could go into at that time.

I've worked with all of the black fraternities and sororities like the Zetas, the Deltas, the Sigma Gammas, the Alphas, and the Omegas. And I've done photographs for most of the churches in Dallas like St. John the Baptist, where I'm a member, Good Street, Salem, Pilgrim's Rest, and New Hope, which is one of the oldest black churches in Dallas.

And I did a lot of work at the city-owned Hilliard golf course in the Love Field area. This was before the airport expanded and it was the only golf course that black people played at. T-Bone Walker would play there with the local golfers when he came to Dallas. There was a social club, an organization. They gave dances too. Whatever they wanted to photograph, they would call me. When I photographed T-Bone Walker there, he was already a celebrity and was living in California.

Most of my work has been in the black community. This is my forty-ninth year as a photographer and I guess the only thing that's gonna make me retire is forgetting how to manipulate the camera properly. I have a dream of publishing a book about the Dallas black community during the period between about 1943 and possibly 1989.

Marion Butts, *American Woodman Special Train*, Dallas, Texas, 1946.

Marion Butts, *Digging the Foundation, Trinity Baptist Church, Reverend C. C. Wright (center)*, Dallas, Texas, 1947.

Marion Butts, *Colonial School*, Dallas, Texas, 1952.

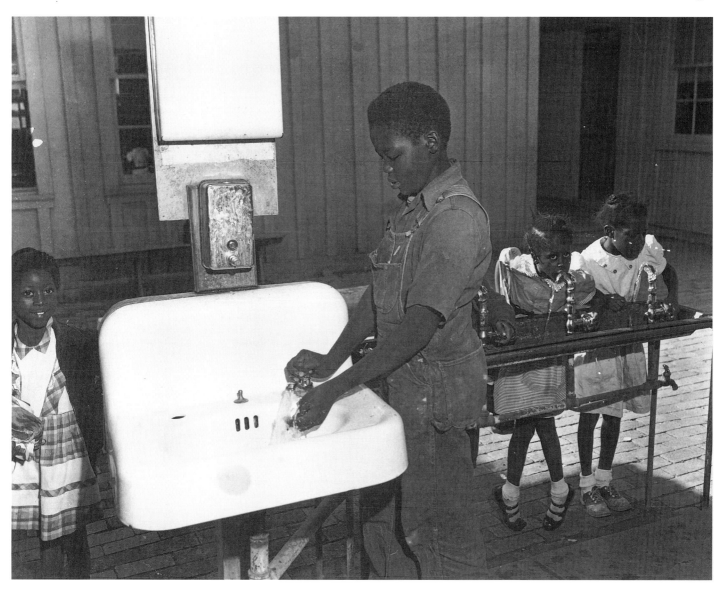

Marion Butts, *Camp Pinkston, Dallas YMCA*, Dallas, Texas, 1965.

Marion Butts, *Dallas Independent School District (for NAACP)*, Dallas, Texas, 1959.

Marion Butts, *NAACP Pickets Skillern's Drugs, (left to right) John Archer Sanders, Charles Garth, E. L. Haywood,* Dallas, Texas, 1961.

Marion Butts, *NAACP Picket, Front row: (left to right) C. Jack Clark, Travis Clark, Roosevelt Johnson; Second row: C. B. Bunkley, unknown, George Allen; Third row: (right) Tony Davis; Fourth row: (right) Pettis Norman; Fifth row: Frank Clark*, Dallas, Texas, 1965.

Marion Butts, *Domino Game in the Boys Department at Moorland Branch YMCA*, Dallas, Texas, 1947.

Marion Butts, *Meditation and Study While Hiking at Camp Pinkston,* Dallas, Texas, 1965.

Marion Butts, *Spiritual Devotion at Camp Pinkston*, Dallas, Texas, 1965.

Marion Butts, *Moorland YMCA Fun at Fundraising Event with Prizefighter Archie Moore*, Dallas, Texas, 1963.

Marion Butts, *U.S. Congressman Adam Clayton Powell of Brooklyn, New York, Guest Speaker at St. John's Baptist Church*, Dallas, Texas, 1963.

Marion Butts, *Press Conference for Thurgood Marshall*, Dallas, Texas, 1954.

Marion Butts, *Buster Smith at the Rose Room*, Dallas, Texas, 1947.

Marion Butts, *S. R. Tankersley Pickets Lincoln Theater for Jobs,* Dallas, Texas, 1949.

Marion Butts, *Colonial School,* Dallas, Texas, 1964.

64

Marion Butts, *Camp Pinkston, Moorland YMCA,* Dallas, Texas, 1965.

Marion Butts, *Dallas YMCA Camp Hunting*, Dallas, Texas, 1946.

Marion Butts, *Dallas Independent School District (for NAACP)*, Dallas, Texas, 1959.

Cato Brown, *James Thibodeaux in Cato Brown's Studio at 2306 Hall Street,* Dallas, Texas, ca. 1950s.

A. B. Bell, *Parade to the State Fair, October 9, 1965*, Dallas, Texas.

A. B. Bell, *Car Ran Thru Cleaners at Chanes Place—High Hill, December 6, 1968*, Dallas, Texas.

A. B. Bell, *Children Playing Handclapping Games*, Dallas, Texas, ca. 1960s.

A. B. Bell, *Church Group*, Dallas, Texas, ca. 1960s.

A. B. Bell, *War on Poverty, September 24, 1966,* Dallas, Texas.

A. B. Bell, *Funeral*, Dallas, Texas, ca. 1960s.

A. B. Bell, *Dunbar Presents Debs, February 19, 1965*, Dallas, Texas.

A. B. Bell, *Cherubim Lodge, Brother Jones and Brother Thomas, August 24, 1965,* Dallas, Texas.

A. B. Bell, *Pearl C. Anderson Queen Ball in Gym, November 17, 1966*, Dallas, Texas.

A. B. Bell, *Man on the Street: Do Negroes Know How to Vote a Split Ticket, Bit O' Africa Room, October 6, 1968,* Dallas, Texas.

George Keaton

I grew up in East Dallas on Carroll Avenue. I was born on October 15, 1933. I went to the Pacific Avenue Elementary until fifth grade, and then to Julia C. Frazier Elementary on Spring Avenue until the eighth grade, and then to Lincoln High School, where I graduated in 1953.

When my uncle, Elvin Frazier, came back from World War II, he brought me four German-made cameras, and he gave them to me, and I got attached to them. My parents were Zeno and Lula Mae Keaton. My dad was born in Mexia and my mother was from Oklahoma. My dad was a waiter at the Adolphus Hotel and my mother did domestic work when I was young. She's eighty-five now and lives with me. My dad died four years ago. He was eighty-one when he died and living in California. My parents split up when I was three or four years old, and he moved to Los Angeles.

I was thirteen or fourteen when I first used the cameras my uncle gave me. At that time, I spent my summers in Oklahoma, where my mother's family lived, and I took pictures of everything I could find in the country: family members, cows, everything. And I sent my film to drugstores for processing and printing.

While I was in school at Lincoln, I started working at Anderson Studio on Oakland Avenue. The photographer was Edwin Anderson, a black photographer. He had been there about four or five years when I got there. He was about twenty-five then. He was a Dallas boy also and he had grown up in South Dallas.

For Anderson, I did all the junior/senior proms, commencement exercises. And after I'd get out of school, I'd go in and print whatever pictures that had been shot during the day. He taught me how to process the film, to print, and to tint the photographs. He showed me practically everything I know. I would process and print all of the black-and-white pictures. There wasn't any color back then.

Anderson taught me how to use a Speed Graphic camera. He owned one himself and he taught me how to use it. You know, I still have that camera and still like it. Anderson worked at the post office, and later he retired. He only did photography part-time. He's an electrician now. He stopped taking pictures about fifteen years ago.

I was drafted into the army in 1954, and when I got out of the service, I started working at a plastic company making skylights and forming plastic. And at night I did nightclub photography. Then on the weekend I'd go back and work at Anderson, and at night I'd be taking nightclubs. I did that for years.

I started working with Joe Johnson about thirty or thirty-five years ago. Johnson went to Lincoln around the same time as me. He was a little ahead of me. We bumped into each other taking pictures. And he'd tag along with me and learn the ropes. We traveled a lot taking pictures. We went to the Zanzibar on Thomas Street, the Empire Room on Hall Street, the Green Cape near the corner of Oakland and Pennsylvania. The Empire Room was owned by Howard Lewis at that time. Big Bo Thomas used to play at the Zanzibar and the touring shows went to the Empire Room—James Brown, Etta James, Bobby Bland, Z. Z. Hill, Chuck Berry, Chubby Checker, Brook Benton, Jackie Wilson, Ray Charles. All the big names were going there back then. Johnny Taylor got his first start at the Empire Room.

Every once in a while I took pictures at the American Woodman Hall at Oakland and Carpenter. They had formal dances there two or three times a month, and they still do. I've been taking pictures for the last thirty-some years. In the 1960s they used to have jazz concerts over there. Fathead Newman played there, and so did James Clay, Buster Smith, and Red Calhoun.

I used my Speed Graphic, and I had to have a motorcycle in those years. And what I would do is to go to a club, park it out front, and come out and let people have their pictures taken on it, like they were riding it. I'd take their name and a number down and deliver the pictures to them the next day. I'd develop them in the morning and then, by noon when I had all of them ready, I'd just go around to where they lived, and deliver them.

I got my first Polaroid camera just after it came out in 1954. I came home on a furlough and picked one up. Then I started taking pictures while I was in the army. I was stationed in El Paso for eighteen months and I went to all the clubs in El Paso taking pictures.

In the clubs I'd go to a booth and see three or four people together and ask them if they wanted a picture. Back then, I was getting just a dollar a print, and then it moved up to two dollars for black-and-white. And that was Polaroid.

I love just taking pictures. I've been doing it and that's all I'm ever going to do. I stopped taking nightclubs ten to fifteen years ago. Now, if I'm at a formal affair, I take an 8x10 Polaroid. You can give a customer an 8x10 color Polaroid in one minute and that's something that none of the other guys have. And I've been doing that for about ten years. Usually, I'd get twelve dollars apiece for color Polaroids.

I haven't always been able to work as a photographer full-time. I worked at Sanger Harris as a salesman in the '60s, and I worked for seventeen years as an apartment manager for Parry Management Company and I worked another ten years for the City of Garland on the weekends as a lifeguard in the summer.

I've only been doing photography full-time for the last twelve years. And my photography continues to improve. I look at some of the older pictures I made years back, and the color has definitely improved. But the black-and-white is still about the same because I still can use my 4x5 camera. The only difference now is that they have a fast film and a slow film. You

George Keaton, *Self-Portrait*, Dallas, Texas, ca. 1950s.

got a Tri X, which is fast, and the Plus X, which is slow. But basically I can do just as well with black-and-white as I did years ago.

My darkroom techniques are still about the same. There's no change in that. I can do the same thing in a darkroom. Eight or ten years ago I dipped into color work in my darkroom, but it didn't seem practical for me because if you got a color setup, you got to be really running a lot of pictures through. If you're shooting one now and one tomorrow, you can't really make it doing your own color. The chemicals have to be at the right temperature, and it's so inexpensive to just take it to a lab now. You can get a volume discount. You can get an 8x10 color print for two dollars. Or you can get ninety-six wallets for ten dollars. So that's a lot better than me trying to print ninety-six wallets in a dark room.

I've only had two studio locations. One was up in the 2700 block of Grand and that was the Parry Management building back then. And I had a studio there for a long time, starting about 1965 or '66. KNOK was in that building and Mr. George Parker told me there was going to be a vacancy. So I came up and put a deposit on it and I guess they held the deposit for three or four months before KNOK moved out. And Mr. Parker was instrumental in me getting that building. He knew the people; he had been there a long time. So I moved in and stayed in there fifteen or sixteen years, until it was bought out seven months ago by Dr. Cowen. I moved when he bought it and six months later they foreclosed on him and my old landlord called me and wanted to know if I would move back. So I decided I would take the building next door. They spent about $19,000 remodeling this building last year. So I'm happy where I'm at right now at 1916 Martin Luther King Boulevard. And I'll be here until I retire.

George Keaton, *Female Vocalist*, Dallas, Texas, ca. 1980s.

George Keaton, *Classic Club*, Dallas, Texas, ca. 1980s.

George Keaton, *"Lil" Joe Blue*, Dallas, Texas, ca. 1980s.

George Keaton, *R. L. Griffin*, Dallas, Texas, ca. 1980s.

Carl Sidle

My interest in photography started when I was a kid. I was born here in Dallas, Texas, in 1943, on November 14th. I was very fortunate. I had a very good family. My mother and father were not rich, but they were together. I lived in the kind of atmosphere that I consider mentally as middle-class, though maybe not economically. I grew up in North Dallas at 1517 Villars Street. It's about a block away from the Board of Education over toward Hall Street, over in that area.

As a kid I remember there was one particular man who used to take quite a few pictures. And my sister was always taking pictures. They both made some kind of impression on my mind early in life.

Later on, I was fortunate to run into the photographer I knew as a child. He's a good friend of mine now. He ended up working a camera in my current neighborhood. One day, he ran into me taking some pictures in Oak Cliff, and we struck up a conversation. Out of the conversation I found out he was the one who had impressed me when I was younger.

His name is Ed White and he doesn't have a studio, but he is employed in the field of photography. He does graphic art works. The last time I talked with him, he was working for Sun Oil, or one of the local companies here. He does weddings at times. I guess he's more or less like me. He's not necessarily out to use photography as a means to make money.

I graduated from Booker T. Washington High School and then I attended Howard University in Washington. I went to Howard in 1962, and unfortunately I didn't graduate. That was during the Vietnam War, and it was a political time in Washington. There were a lot of things that kind of changed my life around at that time. I really got kind of mixed up about

directions. That's one of the unfortunate things in my life. I didn't graduate. I was majoring in mathematics, but I was interested in photography prior to that. I had a roommate who used to take pictures and that caused flashbacks to my childhood. And I guess subconsciously photography was pressing on my mind. The turbulent times in my life during the '60s kind of paralleled the way the country was at that time. Some of the turmoil of the country kind of rubbed off on me, and some of that turmoil evolved from being a black person. There was so much happening mentally and all. And in the process, I found that my direction was missing. I needed some avenue in which I could make some expression. And basically I found that art was a field that was stripped of politics to a certain extent. It was one of the few fields where I felt you could really express yourself without the politics being involved.

I was very much aware of the kind of photography that was done during the Civil Rights era, but in my research on photography, I felt as though the way that I wanted to use it was from an artistic point of view.

The first camera that I used was a Minolta rangefinder. A friend lent it to me, and unfortunately I dropped it once and I damaged it. Now, I work with a Canon A-1 system that I like.

My reason for sticking with 35mm is mostly economics. I just didn't have the money to dabble off in larger formats like I would like to and I could print black-and-white. I don't have my own darkroom. I've always used the darkrooms where I work.

I think that photography has never really been given the kind of credit it is due. I haven't really tried to sell any of my works because I don't want to get into a position where economics or politics is kind of governing what I do. Photography is a hobby in the sense that I do it for enjoyment. I'm currently working for the University of Texas Medical Health Science Center here in Dallas as a medical photographer. I do graphic art works for the doctors and I work in the biochemistry department. I do work that is graphic in nature. I'm involved in working with microscopes and anything to do with doctors having to come up with images pertaining to their work. I've been doing medical photography for fourteen years, since September 14, 1979.

I really didn't start working with a camera until I was thirty-one years old. My reason for wanting to work with a camera was that I was looking for some direction at that point in my life. Deep down inside there was an urge to do something constructive with my life.

So a friend of mine brought a camera by the house and left it. And one day I was looking at it and I thought about taking up photography again. I had help from this friend who was working in a book store, and I began to start reading any kind of books I could on photography. I have never taken any photography courses in my life. My friend's father was a photographer. He became my tutor.

From there, I met Arthello Beck, a local artist in the city. I felt as that if I could take pictures that would please the eyes of an artist, that would lead to some kind of progress in my endeavor to use a camera as an extension of myself.

I'm still striving to become better at using the camera. Most of my works have been oriented toward people. At one time, I did take a lot of pictures of the city of Dallas. And I found that, at that stage, I could work with buildings better than I could with people.

Most of my works are black-and-white; I have some in color, but I tend to like to work in black-and-white as a medium more because it strips the eyes of color and leaves basically the subject matter. To me, black-and-white is a purity of composition.

I enjoy working in the darkroom. I play around with the images. At this particular point in my career, I'm very much interested in learning how to work with graphics on a computer and in manipulating the images to enhance the place of black people in American society and as part of the human race.

And from the time I started until now, I have basically tried to take pictures that convey some positive image of the black community. But I don't just take pictures of black people. I'm really concerned with the positive side of the human spirit.

Carl Sidle, *Junior Black Academy of Arts and Letters Exhibition*, Dallas, Texas, 1990.

Carl Sidle, *Window of Age-Downtown*, Dallas, Texas, 1990.

Carl Sidle, *Bus Ride—Dallas Transit Bus*, Dallas, Texas, 1991.

Carl Sidle, *Untitled*, Dallas, Texas, 1993.

90

Carl Sidle, *Untitled*, Dallas, Texas, 1992.

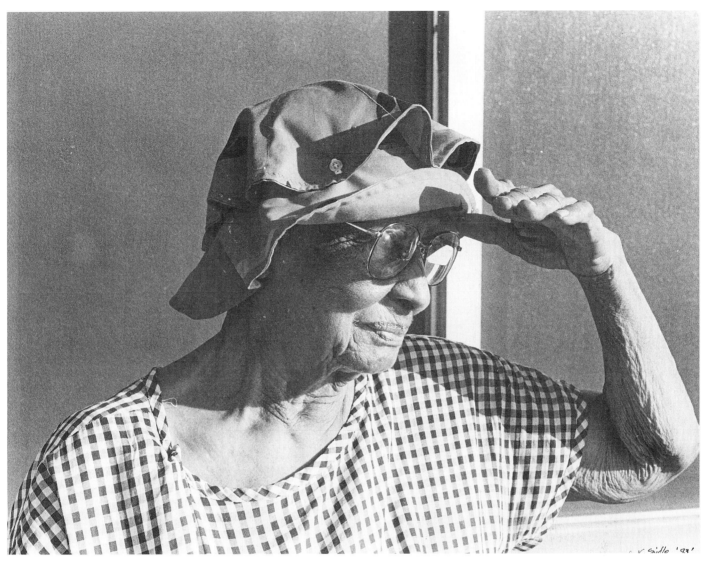

Carl Sidle, *Untitled*, Dallas, Texas, 1993.

Carl Sidle, *Untitled*, Dallas, Texas, 1994.

Carl Sidle, *Untitled*, Dallas, Texas, 1982.

Carl Sidle, *Untitled*, Dallas, Texas, 1993.

Calvin Littlejohn

My grandparents moved to Arkansas from Texas. They were transported from Kentucky down the Mississippi River during slavery time because the Civil War was about to overrun Kentucky and they didn't want to lose the slaves. They transferred them down to the Delta. Texas took them, and my granddaddy eventually made his way up the coast of Texas as a horse trader when he was a teenager. He learned horse trading from the cowboys that he associated with while he was in Texas because he just loved that cowboy stuff, shooting and riding. But he was interested in the finer points of horses and cows—what made a good horse, how do you tell how old he is, how his body was made, and all that kind of thing. So, he saw them doing that in trading, and after he got into the middle of his teenage years, he said, "I think I'll do that myself." He got some horses and cows and took out on his own. He started up the coastline, going from town to town. Saturday was his good day; horses and cows were in demand. But when he got to Texarkana, he heard about some homestead land being available in Arkansas. That claimed his attention, not to buy the land, but to go over there and sell horses. But when he got over there, he found out that you could get a whole section of land for $3,000. And somebody told him, because he didn't read and he couldn't write, that a section was 640 acres. And he decided to buy him a section. He worked hard and made his $3,000 and bought his section of land in the river bottom area of the northeastern part of Arkansas. The river overflowed on that land every spring. That silt would come in there and it was rich as cream. And the part of the land that was high ground had ash wood, gum, pecan, hickory, muscadine, wild grapes, blackberries, pawpaw, persimmon, cypress; all

that was there. And in a young state like Arkansas, lumber was a big thing.

My grandfather said, "I believe I'll farm some of it," and he got out there and cleared up the first forty acres. He got married and started raising children, and he went on and finally ended up clearing 150 acres. He decided to stop there, and his success gained the admiration of the people who had heard about it. He was making a pretty good living and he had some good horses, some cows, and a buggy. Then someone came along and asked, "Do you got any land down there you want to sell?" And he said, "Yeah," and he sold 490 acres and became a wealthy independent black man in that area. We called him D. C. Davie.

I was born on August 1, 1909, in Cotton Plant, Arkansas. When I was nine years old, my mother died, and I got to live with my grandfather. My father disowned me after the death of my mother, and there wasn't nowhere else for me to stay but there. I had some other half-brothers, but their side of the family took them and they went north. My grandfather took me because I was a little bright-eyed boy running around there. And I'd get his shoes and shine them, all that kind of thing. I was at the end of his family. His youngest child was fourteen years older than me. He figured that some day when I grew up, I'd be useful in helping him around the house. He had a good bank account and the equivalent of a Cadillac, which at that time was a surrey with a fringe on top. He had two horses, Alex and Mary. Mary pulled the surrey and Alex pulled the buggy when the time came. And when the preacher came to town, he used that buggy, but his son with all his friends got to use the surrey.

When I was fourteen, my grandfather had an accident. He was a thirty-second degree

Mason and he went to meet some men on a Saturday night, and on his way back about one or two o'clock, his mule fell with him and rammed that horn of the saddle right into his gut and tore him up. He became a semi-invalid. When they brought him home, he couldn't do too much, you know, on the farm. So I had to increase my responsibilities to tend and feed the horses and all that kind of thing. So he decided that living seven miles from town was too far away. He needed to move closer to town, to have some place to stay, where he could go to the doctor. And he bought a twenty-acre piece of land in town with a little house, and remodeled it into a bungalow and moved in. That was in 1924, but then something mysteriously happened. The bank bust, and he lost every cockeyed dime he had, because he had all of his money in the bank.

So we had to borrow money to finish the crop and the largest amount you could borrow was $125. You had to eat on it and you had to feed your horses, unless you could take them out and stake them and let them eat grass. It was incumbent on me at fourteen to take the entire welfare of the family over because his boys were gone. That's where I got my business experience. I had to go and sell a little cotton and I had to make the deal for borrowing the money and putting the hay up and everything. I was in the ninth grade at school, but when all that came about, I had to leave the school in the month of March to go and come back and start preparing my land. Consequently, I never could finish a school year. I stayed in the ninth grade four years.

Well, my granddaddy saw what was happening. I was getting older. I was eighteen, and he said, "Tell you what you do, you're not going to make enough money here to go to school. Just leave and go get you a job and make you some money, and just leave us here; and if you do that, some of it will come back." And that's what I did. Went down the street and worked for the Childress family for five dollars a week with room and board and made enough money to pay tuition for one semester at Philander Smith College. I went there and didn't know what was going to happen when I got there. And it was at Philander Smith that my interest in photography began. At that time I had no skills for photography, but I had taken a correspondence course in

Calvin Littlejohn, *Self-Portrait*, Fort Worth, Texas, ca. 1950s.

commercial art, and there was a segment on graphic art that led me into photography.

I was on my way to the movie theater and happened to look through the door in this warehouse nearby. I hadn't really ever seen inside a studio. I just stood there motionless; I don't know how long. They were doing sketching for the theater prosceniums and I said to myself, "Oh, you can do this and then get money for it?" And I stood there so long that one of them came over and they introduced themselves as Fats and Slats. One of them was fat and one of them was thin and tall. So one of them said "Boy, you like this work?" and I said, "Yes, sir. Can I come in and watch you work?"

"Yes, you can come on in here if you don't get in the way," and I just stood against the wall and watched them all that day 'til my time ran out and I had to go back to my little domestic job. So, naturally, when I had a little time, I ran back down there again. And I'd watch them, and I'd stand around, but I'd always make myself useful while I was around there. If I saw something like trash that could be swept up or something that could be moved for their advantage, I'd just do it, and they'd say, "Oh, yeah. We got ourselves a new janitor."

So one day, it was on a Wednesday, I believe it was, they were running behind. And they had a sketch layout of Dr. Fu Manchu on a 4x8 Epson board on the easel there. They had the paints already made. It was an eight-tone composition and they were at the far end of the building putting together some props. So, I said to myself, "Let me see if I can't fill in these. That's all I'm going to do." I grabbed one of them sable brushes and I went crazy. And when they turned around I was almost through with it. It's not permissible for me to say what they said then, but anyway, "We've got us a helper." Then they started trying to figure out how I was going to help them. That was the problem, because you had to be a member of the union at that time. In 1933, there was no chance for me to join the union, you see. But they figured it out. They went down and complained to the boss that they needed more money. They just had to have more money. And when they got the money they cashed it and they throwed it off to me and that's the way I got paid.

I worked with them off and on for about three years, but while I was going to and forth for them, I sought the opportunity to get some more work. And I passed right by the Kitterand Professional Photo Studio going in on a vacant lot between the studio and a warehouse. I didn't pay it any attention until one day I saw that there was a great big 8x10 picture, and I knew a professional artist had to put the inscriptions on pictures like that for conventions. So I went in there and asked for the job and got it. That's where the bug bit me, when I got in there.

I said, "Is this kind of similar to graphic arts? Mr. Kitterand, what's the difference?" And he said, "Well, this is a continuous tone. Come on back here and let me show you."

I went on back there and he started showing me about posing and lights and shadows. I had studied that until the nth degree in art, you know. So he said, "Maybe you can help me some time." And I just kind of drifted off that way. Shortly after that, my job played out with the domestic people there. The people I was working for decided to move to Fort Worth and

when they decided to move, I started looking and I couldn't find a regular job because in such a little city all the jobs were taken up. So I asked him, "Can I go to Texas with you and look for something there?" And that's how I hoboed to Fort Worth with them. I came in the car with them. I called it hobo, but it wasn't, because I had the promise that I could at least live with them until I found some place to work because they didn't need me. So I came on and lived with them and was paid the same horrendous salary that they had paid me in Arkansas: $3.50 a week, room, and board.

When I got to Fort Worth, Mrs. R. C. Bright, the lady who brought me with her family, said that I should learn how to cook better so that I could get a job cooking. So I took her advice and took her recommendation and went to a cooking school in Como to get a certificate in cooking. Then I tried to get a job as a cook.

I worked for the Cranes as a nurse, cook, and chauffeur at $8 a week, and stayed in the servants' quarters. And one Saturday I was cleaning up the house and looked in the closet. I took everything out and found a portrait of her grandfather or somebody. And I was just standing in the middle of the floor looking at it when Mrs. Crane came through.

"What are you doing looking at that?"

"Mrs. Crane, I was just admiring this because I am a painter."

And she said, "You're too ambitious."

I put everything back and two weeks after that I was fired and out in the street. I went back to Mrs. U. S. Smith and asked her to help me get a job. She said, "Where are you going to stay?" And I said, "I don't have anywhere to stay."

"Well stay here with me and be my cook for a few days until I find you a job."

So she did; she got me a job cooking out on a ranch for about two weeks. They wanted somebody to cook because their mother was sick. Two weeks after that, she died and they didn't need me. I went back to Mrs. Smith and said, "Mrs. Smith, I got to make something on my own. I can't keep running around like this. I'm going to rent a place in your basement and I'm going to paint landscapes; and your son, he doesn't have a job either, he knows the town. I'll let him sell them." So I started painting and accumulated a little money. Both of us made a

Calvin Littlejohn, *Baseball Player (Littlejohn Studio, Sponsor),* Fort Worth, Texas, ca. 1940s.

little money, and then her son said, "Mr. Littlejohn, I'm going to introduce you to the city."

Well, the pictures kind of introduced me first and an art teacher at an elementary school on Clinton Avenue asked me to help her with her class in preparation for a poster contest. I didn't know to what extent I could help them, but I knew I was going to try to make them do the best they could. And so I carried them through. I put a lot of heavy stuff in them: sketching, lettering, color balance, and sketching action. I sent them to the window and taught them how to look at some person and catch just one action—throwing a ball or something—just freeze it right there in your mind. Come back to the board and put it on the board in crayon or chalk. "After you get the stick figure up there, the head and all that kind of thing, now dress it up. Put a shirt and collar on it."

So when they placed their work in the contest at the bank, it shot over the high school. Actually this high school didn't come anywhere near what they had done in the elementary school. Then they started asking, "Who was it that helped you?" And that gave me a job as a professor within the industrial department of the city of Fort Worth under G. B. Trimble. I taught art, and after I was with him awhile, the academic faculty saw my work and transferred me out to a regular school. They put all of the black artists in the city of Fort Worth over here at Quinn, and that's how I started there. Now I taught there awhile, and then I saw a need for photography because the I. M. Terrell High School was having trouble getting photography to make the yearbooks and things. The city of Fort Worth had one photographer on payroll, and he just couldn't make it to all of the schools. I. M. Terrell was being neglected a lot. So I went to them with a proposition that I could be the photographer if I could get some equipment.

I worked in a white photographic studio until I could get some equipment. I started there, and I adopted that school and they

Calvin Littlejohn, *Fat Stock Show*, Fort Worth, Texas, ca. 1947.

adopted me, and that's how I got into photography.

I opened the Littlejohn Studio in 1934, and I just carried that name from then on; not at the same location, though. My first location was in my little quarters where I lived on Ninth Street. I lived in the same place, upstairs. I lived there; I made the pictures there. I had my little cot, and I had a screen that Dr. Flint gave me. I put a blanket over it when customers came in. Then I found out it was hard even for me to make enough money to pay the rent there and pay the notes on my cameras and support myself on what I was making. I was the only professional black photographer that had been in Fort Worth that anyone could remember. People were not orientated in going to a black photographer. Only thing they wanted was just some little old snapshot or stand up against a wall and shoot. And that's it. But it was hard for me to get them to understand that you could pay more than fifty cents for the professional end of it.

For the school work I used a Ricohflex 2¼x2¼ camera. Then I bought a B&W Press King 4x5 camera from Camera Craft. That's when I got interested in going into picture packaging, and that almost ran me nuts. I didn't have a system.

My darkroom was in my bathroom. And I put together my own enlarger with the same camera. I went into somebody's kitchen and got me two dish pans and made my lamp, inverted them together, made a lamp house, put a light in there, went to the camera shop and got some opaque diffuser, put it between the light and the film, made a gadget where I could hook it together, and made my own thing that I could slide up and down. I used the camera as the lens in the enlarger, the camera that I photographed with.

You know, when you got to do it, you got to do it. I can tell you a whole lot of engineering things. I didn't learn all that, it had to be done, and I just did it. And after I got that going, I got more work.

One of my biggest contracts was in 1941. A preacher came in. He was a very flamboyant preacher from St. James Church, and he wanted to get known to the public and everything. So he called me and says, "Come over here, Littlejohn. I want you to be here at morning service and make some pictures of me at the church. And I want 150 pictures of me by 3:00 today, 5x7 size." I delivered. I got my first manufactured enlarger just before I went into the service. I got an old enlarger from a boy from the Fort Worth *Press.* I can't think of the name of it, but the diffuser was the lens itself. And as long as you keep it clean, you can't beat it. I took it through the service with me. Brought it back and it's out there with the rest of my stuff.

I have a couple of Speed Graphic cameras and they are fifty years old or more. And I got the Konica and I got the Canon and I got a camera I use for the schools.

The Konica used 127 roll film. But I like to work with as large a negative as I possibly can. And I can go up to 4x5. And I do that sometimes. And then I bought a Corona Rollback, which uses 70mm film, and it fits on the 4x5 camera. So it contains 100 feet of film and it has 320 possible exposures. Then I got a Beedipotronic camera that used 46mm film for schoolwork and I discovered a way to get 640 exposures instead of 320.

I also invented something else, known as the Plantation Printer. It's a great big thing, and when I expose that 46mm film, I put it on this and I can put five frames in at one time and expose five frames. Each frame is scientifically balanced for light according to the density of its negative. I invented that. With this, I could print a lot faster, and my wife and I could keep pace with my competitors in Wolfe City, just the two of us, and he had twenty-six working with him.

Hennington was a white photographer in Wolfe City. We came out of the service about the same time, and he invited me to see his plant. I had to stay in there to beat the competition. I could print one thousand kids in three hours.

I've done school work. I've done documentaries. I've done work for my magazine. I published a magazine here in 1947. It was called *Spot,* but I went broke in one year.

In 1947 I went to the Southwestern and Texas Professional Photographers Association meeting. The convention was held April 28, 29, 30, and May 1 at the Texas Hotel and blacks were not allowed to go up the front elevator in prime time. And this was the first time blacks were allowed to go up the front elevator, because I asked and they let me. There was only one other black photographer at the convention and that was Teal from Houston. He was one of our state's best. I got a lot of confidence from him. He was my main man. He used to come here and do all the big ones before I learned to do them.

Teal was friendly with a lot of community people in Dallas and in Fort Worth, where he would visit and make pictures because there wasn't a black photographer there. One of the first pictures of his that I saw was an 11x14 print hanging over the principal's office in the elementary school in Lake Como. That's a little black community west of Fort Worth. And as I looked at the picture, I admired it and asked questions about who made it. Well, that stuck in my mind, and then I began to read the papers and found out about his activity in Dallas. He was friends with an architect named Hardy, and when he came to Fort Worth, he lived with Hardy on Terrell Street. Hardy would drum up the business in the community for Teal, and when Teal got to Fort Worth he'd either work in Hardy's house or in the homes of his clients. He didn't have a studio here, and that's the way he operated. And after a little while, I learned how to do it. What I learned from Teal was his gift of communication.

I did a lot of news photography. Whenever Carter Wesley had a story in Fort Worth, he'd send one of his people, and the guy that I used as my editor for my magazine wrote for him. His name was Robert Gregory. He's dead now. Everybody called him "Bob."

During that time black newspapers were not a lucrative market for photography because they couldn't pay you that much. Mostly the stuff that you did for them was just gratis for publicity. You gave them a picture and they put it in there with the credit, photo by Littlejohn. But I couldn't cash that at the bank. So I decided I needed some way to make a living. That's why I specialized in the schools. Then I minimized my weddings and things like that because I was running around buying materials and doing schools around in the state, down in Jefferson, Texas, and East Texas and around like that. But every once in awhile, I'd get an assignment to do some news photography.

I was the only black photographer in this area. I was here and I was the only one who elected to starve to make a job out of it. There were some others who I helped along the way. John Turner was one, but he's dead now.

When I first came to Fort Worth, I worked part-time in a white studio. I knew the price, but then when I came back to my people, I had work with a different economic stratum. And I made prices on the basis of that. In the 1930s I would have gotten in my car and driven to Dallas for a dollar a picture, go from house to house. For 8x10 commercial pictures, not portraiture, I sold them for fifty cents. After the war, I went to seventy-five cents, then a dollar, then a dollar and a half, and my black-and-white never did go beyond that in a commercial vein. I charge by the sitting now and it's reasonable, very reasonable.

I did some work for the Kansas City *Call*, the Fort Worth *Eagle Eye*, a little for the Chicago *Defender*, and even the Fort Worth *Star Telegram*. But the *Star Telegram* had a thing that at that time they weren't publishing very many pictures of black people. Consequently, there wasn't any demand. I did, however, cover when the big bands came here for the local papers: Duke Ellington, Cab Calloway, Jimmy Lunceford, Louis Jordan, Roy Milton, and all those guys. But I could only submit photographs when they played for the white audiences. If they didn't I could still submit the pictures, but they wouldn't print them. Do you hear what I'm talking about?

I did some work for the NAACP. I say work for them, but not so far as getting money for it or anything like that. Naturally, I'm a member and have been a member for a number of years. And I'd make pictures for them every time they came here. I did a portrait of Harold Flowers. He was at Philander Smith at the same time as me. He was a grade ahead of me, and he emerged as one of the greatest civil rights lawyers in Arkansas.

In addition to photography, I did some painting. Dr. Pinkston's family commissioned me to do a portrait of him, and they hung it at the school that was named after him. The painting was made from a schematic from a black-and-white photograph.

I have about forty thousand negatives in my collection, I guess, something like that. My prime concern was just making a living. I had to sell it, you understand. I didn't go out and document it unless somebody employed me. One time, though, I was right up here on Evans in my studio. And I heard a shot and I went out and grabbed my camera. I walked out and right in front of the cafe, about two or three doors from where my studio was on this street, they were bringing a man out that was dead on a stretcher. And I shot it. But I didn't go out just looking for something like that.

Another time, in 1946, I heard a bomb go off. At four o'clock in the morning I heard this loud explosion. I got up, grabbed my camera, and started toward it. I saw that somebody had placed a bomb under a black man's side of a house. It was near the bathroom and it had blown all that side off. And when I made pictures of that, I submitted them to the NAACP. The contention was that the man had crossed into an area that was supposed to be all white. They had put out all kinds of signs, "Niggers not wanted down here," and every once in a while they would stage Ku Klux Klan symbolism, have kids with white bags over their faces and crosses marching around.

In the early days, Negroes didn't have any hospital to go to. So St. Joseph's Hospital permitted black patients in the basement. You walked down there and you stepped over something and you went down to the basement. Well, Mr. Percy Walker's daughter was operated on, and he was sitting up with her one night. It was about one o'clock or one-thirty in the morning, and he noted that something fell on the floor. He looked over in the corner and a big piece of plaster had fallen out of the ceiling. And about the time he straightened up, he looked up and the whole ceiling was cracking. He figured it was going to fall on his daughter and he ran to the bed, but before he could get there all that stuff fell right down on top of them, and a metal pipe hit him right across the back and knocked him down on top of her. And he struggled to his knees and finally got her out. And he came over to my studio and knocked on the door at four o'clock in the morning. I always slept in my studio to make

Calvin Littlejohn, *Lucretiah Littlejohn Tinting Photographs at Littlejohn Studio, 1057 Evans,* Fort Worth, Texas, ca. 1950s.

ends meet, and I went to the door. He said, "Littlejohn, would you come over to St. Joseph's Hospital to help me build a case?" So I rushed over there in my '47 Ford, and just grabbed my camera and stuck my bulb in there and started shooting. Well, that attracted the attention of the nurses, and about the time I got to the door to leave, they were bearing down on me. So I ran and jumped over that thing to get to my car and crank it up. I didn't know whether or not it would crank up, but it did just before they got to me. It was like somebody was knocking on the windows. But I went on and developed the film. Ordinarily, you would get some legal recognition or something, but that case stayed in litigation for four or five years and was never settled. And Percy died from that lick across there.

I took a lot of pictures for the NAACP. I did it at the Safeway store right down the street here. In a community like this, you would think if a store opened, it'd be nice to employ some of the people that were capable who lived in the community, especially since they were paying a pretty good price. That didn't happen. So the NAACP sent a man in there to organize a protest and for that protest, they needed some pictures and I was forbidden to make pictures. But I made them anyway with the car running at forty miles an hour—hit and run.

I've got all my negatives, but they got all messed up for several reasons. When I was in the studio down on Bryan Street, the burglars got so bad I had to move. They came in here looking for different things, and I had them boxes put in order. And when they came in, they'd just turn them over and I just never had a chance to go back and organize them. I had to just take a shovel in many cases and scoop them up and then put them in the boxes. Some I have organized pretty good, but most of them, it would take days and weeks to kind of line them up so I could recognize them. With the ongoing work of making a living, I don't have much time to turn back what's not actual money.

Calvin Littlejohn, *Lucretiah Littlejohn with a Client at Littlejohn Studio,* 1057 Evans, Fort Worth, Texas.

Calvin Littlejohn, *Joe Louis (center)*, Fort Worth, Texas, ca. 1950s.

Calvin Littlejohn, *Ella Fitzgerald*, Fort Worth, Texas, ca. 1950s.

Calvin Littlejohn, *Dickerson Beauty School Commencement, October 31, 1948*, Fort Worth, Texas.

Calvin Littlejohn, *Adam Clayton Powell (center) at a Reception*, Fort Worth, Texas, ca. 1950s.

Calvin Littlejohn, *Oscar Peterson Trio*, Fort Worth, Texas, ca. 1950s.

Calvin Littlejohn, *Jackie Robinson (left), Lucretiah Littlejohn, Roy Campanella*, Fort Worth, Texas, ca. 1950s.

Curtis Humphrey

I came to Tyler in December 1947 to be an instructor of photography at Texas College. I came from Wiley College and I've been here ever since.

I was born on December 14, 1907. I grew up in Dirgin, Texas, a small place in Rusk County between Henderson and Tatum. In my immediate family there were two sets of children. There were eight total, on my immediate side and on my half side. I'm pretty much in the middle. My dad was a farmer, and he was the type of person who could do almost anything. I

Curtis Humphrey, *Self-Portrait*, Tyler, Texas, ca. 1960s.

left home because I didn't have a chance to go to school past the fifth grade. I was promoted to the sixth, but I had to work. My parents were old and poor. We lived in the backwoods, and I didn't have any money. So I just wanted to make me a little money. So I'd do little odd jobs. I'd cut cord wood and pick cotton or do whatever to make a little money. I lived there until I was sixteen, and then I decided I wanted to get out for myself, and I got a job working on the railroad. I worked in wiring in beds and filling in the trestles. It wasn't motorized, but it was "mule-ized," if anyone still knows what a mule is. Well, I worked on the railroad for two years and I moved on and started traveling around, just riding freight trains and different things like that. I got odd jobs doing construction, and then I went to working for department stores. I had a little talent. I could build different things and make display things for the store windows. I just had a talent to do those kind of things and never had a problem getting a job. So I worked for them until I decided to move on. Then I started to work for a grain door factory that was making grain doors for box cars. And I watched the guy running his machine and he asked me if I wanted to try it. And I told him, "Yes." So he gave me the job running the edger. Well, I worked for him for about a year or so and I decided to change again and went to Fort Worth and that's when I started into photography.

I was working at a shoe store for two brothers. One of the brothers was the manager, and the other was named Harry Berkman. Well, Berkman and another guy from Pennsylvania named Harry Garonzik got together to take pictures on the street. And at that time everything was pretty slow. Wages were cheap and everything else. So one of the guys asked my manager if it would be okay for me to work half a day for him and half a day at the store. Well, we agreed and after about three weeks of watching him process negatives to be shown the next day, he gave me a key to the place. And I decided I was going to try to do what he was doing. So I went out and bought me some extra supplies and tried it. Well, it didn't look too good to me. So I waited another week and that time it came out good and I left it. And when he came in, he asked me who had done this work, and I told him I did. He said, "Who told you how?"

I said, "I was watching you."

He said, "You were watching me and did it that good?"

"Yeah."

He said, "Well, in about a month I'm going to let you take over here, and I'll get out on the road."

And that's how it happened. That was in 1932. After I got into photography, the guy went out on the road and set up in different places. So it got a little heavy for me, and I sent for my brother and got him to go to Dallas to work. And when it got a little heavier, I sent and got another brother, and later, I sent for one of my cousins. Then I said, "I think I'll go in for myself."

My brothers were Vernon and Dewitt. We lost Vernon in a fire in Dallas. My cousin was a Barr, but he never became a photographer. He only worked in processing. Dewitt worked for a long time as a photographer in Dallas. He set up on the south side and I set up on the north side.

When I worked in Dallas, it was pretty rough. And the Central Tracks was the roughest of all. I didn't mess around too much around that area. I was located at the corner of Thomas and Hall. I did what you might call street soliciting. I had a guy that would go out and solicit customers and they'd come in and get portraits. And then we'd do street pictures, you know. You'd be walking down the street and I would snap your picture and give you a card and you could come in. And we'd send each other customers.

I met the photographer Teal in Dallas in the '30s. We were competitors then. I had just gotten started when I met him. I think we just bumped into each other at some kind of special occasion, and that was the first and only time I really remember ever seeing him. I had heard the name "Teal," but I didn't know anything about him. I had probably been operating about a year when I met him. In fact, I think some of his associates or students had visited here one time. They stopped in and talked with me awhile. There was another black photographer they called Littlejohn, I believe. I don't remember meeting him. He was in Fort Worth. I left Dallas in 1942 and went into the air force.

I was stationed at McDill Field in Tampa, and also at Andrew Field. They're pretty close together. I got to be the photographer for the base paper. They wouldn't let me ship out. So they fixed me a lab on base, and at first they didn't think they could get the equipment they needed. They needed an enlarger and they couldn't get one. So I told them, I'd make one.

I said, "Get me a lens and a lamp house, and I can use the camera for the bellows."

So he said, "Draw up the specifications and we'll get it made."

Well, I drew it up, and he made it. It worked good, but it was slow. And about a week or two after that, he got me an enlarger. But I never used the light meter. And one day he asked me if I wanted to use his light meter and I told him, "For what?"

He said, "How are you going to know how to make your exposure?"

And I said, "Well, I'm looking at it."

So when I got through setting it up, I said, "Check it," and he checked it with his meter, and he said, "I don't believe it." So, I didn't need the meter. I could read the light according to what I was used to and calculate the exposure.

The first camera I had was called a Pack camera because the film came in packs. The negatives were 3¼ x 4¼, and the next camera I got was a DeVry movie camera that was geared to single shots. A lot of my other equipment I designed myself.

After I was discharged from the service I got a Speed Graphic camera. That was when I moved to Marshall to teach at Wiley College. They wanted to put in a photography class and asked me if I would teach it.

Then I went to Texas College to teach photography in 1947. There had been another photographer at Texas College before I got there. His name was W. B. Harris. He was out of Kilgore. He wrote insurance and did photography on the side. And somehow he drowned at the Lake of the Pines.

I taught in a temporary program at Texas College for veterans of the war. But everything eventually changed in that area. Now during that time a high school student could teach on a high school certificate, but later they stopped that. I had the lowest education of any person teaching photography. Some people came here from Austin and they interviewed me and I told them that I had been promoted to the sixth grade. They didn't believe it, especially when I told them about the chemistry and the math part of photography.

Well, my class went out in about 1952, and I've been in this building on North Grand since 1954. I've done portraits, any kind of pictures that the people wanted. There was only one other black photographer working here in East Texas when I got here. I don't know when he got into it. I can't think of his name. I think he was in Mineola.

As time went on, I got other cameras. In 35mm, I had a Leica. Today, I use Minolta, Pentax, and Canon, and sometimes I still use larger format cameras. For enlargers, I used mostly the Omega for black-and-white, and the Besseler for color. The equipment for color was a little more expensive than I wanted at the time, but a guy told me that I couldn't do it, and I told him that I could. So that's the reason I went into color processing myself. I used to do a lot of hand-coloring and -tinting.

I did a lot of school work before integration, and since integration I haven't been out. I lost my wife in 1960 and it's been hard for me to travel as much as I used to. I used to work in all the black schools in a two-hundred-and-fifty-mile radius.

I have taught maybe one or two to be photographers. There's one in Wichita Falls. His name is Reginald Robinson, and there's another who went to Louisiana, somewhere outside of Shreveport. I can't think of his name now. He was one of my early students.

When I was traveling around I used to charge a dollar a shot for black-and-white. Well, my prices have increased quite a bit. They went up and down. Actually, black-and-white's a lot higher than color right now because of the chemistry. It takes more silver in black-and-white than color.

When I first started I made bromide prints. I used to weigh all of my chemicals myself. Now, you buy it already mixed and all you do is follow the directions and dilute it. A lot has changed.

I stay as busy as I want to, sometimes more. I live about a mile from my studio. I have five children, and a couple of them are trying to do something in photography. Richard and Gail. She's married again. They're my baby boy and baby girl. Gail's twenty-nine, and Richard's thirty-seven.

I do most of my photography work here. I do weddings out, but the portraits I do in my studio. I have a partner in my business. His name is Alan Jones Jr. and he's about forty-eight years old. He started with me in 1972. He wasn't a student of mine. He was just kind of curious and started working with a Polaroid.

I've taken lots of pictures around Tyler. I'd go to all kinds of social functions. I even took photographs out at the Western Foundry. I went out there just because I wanted to do something. That was back in the '50s. I wasn't planning to stay no time, but I just wanted to see what it was like. I photographed parades, graduations, and churches, such as the St. Mary's Baptist Church, Mile High Chapel, all the churches around.

I even went from here to San Antonio to do weddings. I did a little bit of work in Austin in the '30s. My contact has always been people who knew me in different areas. I've done pictures in South Texas, and as far away as Iowa, Georgia, Florida, the Carolinas, Washington, and New York. I've gone for as long as months at a time. I never located there. I got recommendations from people. I never advertised through any media or newspapers.

The best film I have found for black people is higher speed. High-speed film is more sensitive to all colors and higher-contrast paper is better for black people. I only used selenium or sepia toning when I was going to color the picture. The toning made the colors blend in better.

One time I went to a supply place to buy some paper. They didn't have the type I asked for, and I said, "You know I can't use bromide on us."

And he laughed and asked, "Why?"

I said, "Because it makes us too white and y'all too black." I've learned this through experience.

Sometimes when I'm printing I use diffusers. You can buy diffusers of all different natures, but the best diffuser I ever came across was the cellophane on a cigarette pack. It makes one of the best diffusers. It changes the direction of the light rays. I'd use it when I did a lot of retouching and I didn't want the retouch to show up. It helps sometimes with old people who have a lot of wrinkles.

I've done all kinds of photography. I've done businesses, policemen, car and truck wrecks. I've gone to funerals and cemeteries. Sometimes I'd get called to take pictures of the body in the funeral home or the church because some member of the family couldn't be there and wanted to see the deceased.

Once when I first got started taking pictures of these bodies, they had one that was in the house, in a home. And I had a little old rickety tripod. So there I was, and the body was in one of those cheap caskets. The head was so low down in there that I couldn't see it too good. So

nobody was there but me, and I looked around and found a book, a Bible that was pretty thick. I reached down there and picked his head up and stuck that book underneath and took his picture. And when I was done I took the book from under his head and put it back.

On several occasions I had to make some adjustments to get the picture. Sometimes I had to take pictures of bodies that had autopsies done of them because the person had been shot, or something like that. Usually, those were for lawyers.

I threw a lot of my old negatives away. I just didn't have anywhere to put them. I didn't start a good filing system until about the mid-1970s. I never did quit taking pictures. I was making more taking pictures on the weekend than I was out there hustling all week. I'm just curious. I just want to keep at it. That's about the best that I know.

Curtis Humphrey, *Wedding*, Tyler, Texas, ca. 1960s.

Curtis Humphrey, *Kindergarten Graduation*, Tyler, Texas, ca. 1950s.

Curtis Humphrey, *Delta Sigma Theta Sorority,* Tyler, Texas, ca. 1970s.

Curtis Humphrey, *East Texas Ranch*, Tyler, Texas, ca. 1970s.

Curtis Humphrey, *Graduation Procession, Jarvis Christian College,* Hawkins, Texas, ca. 1970s.

Curtis Humphrey, *Duck Hunters,* Tyler, Texas, ca. 1970s.

Curtis Humphrey, *Coronation,* Tyler, Texas, ca. 1960s.

Curtis Humphrey, *The Gala Club, Annual Spring Ball*, Tyler, Texas, ca. 1970s.

Curtis Humphrey, *Funeral*, Tyler, Texas, ca. 1960s.

Curtis Humphrey, *Gravesite*, Tyler, Texas, ca. 1960s.

Curtis Humphrey, *Teenage Girl*, Tyler, Texas, ca. 1970s.

Curtis Humphrey, *Wedding*, Tyler, Texas, ca. 1970s.

Curtis Humphrey, *Church Service*, Tyler, Texas, ca. 1970s.

Curtis Humphrey, *Old Ironsides*, Tyler, Texas, ca. 1960s.

Curtis Humphrey, *Funeral*, Tyler, Texas, ca. 1960s.

Curtis Humphrey, *Standing Man*, Tyler, Texas, ca. 1950s.

Curtis Humphrey, *Professor, Texas College,* Tyler, Texas, ca. 1960s.

Curtis Humphrey, *Singers*, Tyler, Texas, ca. 1970s.

Pearlie B. Roquemore

Eugene Roquemore and I were married about twenty-two years, from 1972 to his death on March 30, 1993. At the time that we met, he was working at the bus station part-time and at Frito-Lay full-time. And he was a photographer just whenever he needed to make a picture—at the church, or a social group or at schools. Different ones called him. He made family pictures all the time. He got interested in making pictures when he was in the military service, and after he was discharged he went to Wiley College to learn to be a photographer. He was born in Timpson, Texas, on February 3, 1921, the third-born of nine children, but lived in Henderson until he moved to Lubbock in 1952.

I was born on March 14, 1922, in Navarro County, near Corsicana, Texas. I was reared about twenty-one miles from there in a little place called Wortham. That's where I spent my childhood days and high school and all of that.

I heard about Blind Lemon Jefferson when I was just a little girl, before I started to school. I started school when I was seven years old. I heard how he could, they called it pick the guitar and sing the blues. What they were saying was the blues. My daddy said they were reels. He was a Baptist preacher and he said if a song wasn't spiritual or gospel, it was a reel. And the reels were ugly things to listen to. He called it the devil's music. And of course, growing up, he wouldn't let us listen to that. I had to get up and go to school before I really heard Blind Lemon pick that guitar and sing those ugly songs.

I remember seeing him when I was a little bitty girl, at I don't know what occasion it was, but we would go to this church and they would have something like a picnic. And I remember seeing Blind Lemon playing his guitar, setting in a chair, and people were standing around listening. I understand he did sing religious songs, but at first, when I first heard about him, my daddy said he was singing devil's songs, so those weren't church songs.

I came from Wortham, Texas, on a cotton pick, cotton pull or whatever; they were pulling cotton. And my mother's twin sister lived here in Lubbock. And I come home with her. We stayed in Idaloo for a month during the cotton-pulling season, and after that we moved to Lubbock. My aunt bought a house over on Ivory Street. And I first came to visit her in September of 1943. But it wasn't until 1953 that I moved to Lubbock myself.

Lubbock was famous for growing cotton at that time. It was really a treat for me to learn how to pull cotton. I'd never pulled cotton before. And when I come out to Lubbock, I started pulling cotton for the first year I was here with my aunt that lived in Idaloo.

I didn't know anything about photography when I got to Lubbock. I didn't become acquainted with it until we had to have pictures made at different occasions at school. And that's when I got to know the Roberts Studio.

When Eugene got to Lubbock, he worked at the Roberts Studio. Sam Roberts was a white photographer. He had a studio downtown, where the First National Bank has its parking lot now. And when I met Eugene, he was working out of Mr. Roberts's studio in addition to his jobs at Frito-Lay and the bus station.

We got along real fine with Mr. and Mrs. Roberts. Whenever they'd have birthday parties or anything like that, they'd invite us to them and we went. And when sometimes it wasn't a special occasion Mrs. Roberts would cook and invite us over to eat. And she'd come out here and make pictures for us.

Mr. and Mrs. Roberts were good to Eugene

Eugene Roquemore, *Photography Class Taught by Curtis Humphrey at Wiley College*, Marshall, Texas, ca. 1947.

and me. Mr. Roberts died around 1970, and his wife took it over. Then she sold the studio to Toni. I don't remember her last name, but she worked for Mr. Roberts too. And after Toni died, her niece took over the business, and her niece finally sold it and moved to Dallas. And what happened to the studio then, I don't know. At that time Eugene was working at Frito-Lay full-time and at the bus station part-time. But his health was getting bad. He had to have his first surgery in 1976.

During the 1950s and '60s, blacks and whites were pretty separate. I remember when they integrated here. I remember before Eugene and I married; I lived right across from the high school, the only high school, the black high school. Now, it's a junior high. They just made it a junior high last year, this year [1994]. In Lubbock, it was just about like it was in most other places, as far as I'm concerned.

After they integrated the school, I remember

one incident so well. Some boy shot and killed one of the students over at Dunbar [High School] which was across from my house. And I had to leave home because there were helicopters and tanks. Everything else broke down and people were chasing each other, running round. You were just afraid to be at home. Yes, sir. The police shot through a house, through one of my houses. And they had children—well, this boy, whoever he was, had shot at this policeman or something. It was a black boy. And he ran into these folks' house and the police were in a tank at that time. That was in the '70s. I think a white student killed a black student at school. That's what happened. The school was newly integrated and it caused a lot of unrest.

Sometimes they called Eugene to the school to make school pictures, and when the Masonic people would have their annual whatever it was, parade or day, he would make pictures for

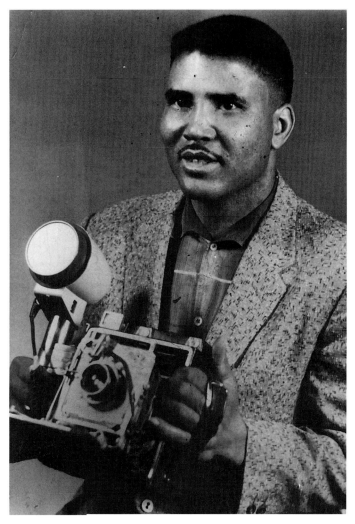

Eugene Roquemore, *Self-Portrait*, Lubbock, Texas, ca. 1960s.

them. And he made pictures for church groups. And sometimes birthday parties and picnics and things like that.

Eugene took pictures at the Cotton Club before my time. And I don't know where he went. I remember him telling me about an incident that happened at the Cotton Club one time that he was there. From what I could gather, he was there to make a picture for somebody and some man got to shooting and he had to run off and leave his camera to get up under a table, to get away from gunfire.

I really don't know too much about the Cotton Club. I just heard about the Cotton Club. I never went there. As I said, in '53 when I moved to Lubbock, having been taught all of my life that dance places were the wrong place to go, I didn't go to the Cotton Club. I heard about it, but never saw it. Now, Eugene showed

me pictures that he made of the Cotton Club—like people sitting at the tables and people on the floor dancing and stuff like that. But that was before my time.

Eugene used a big camera, a portrait camera, and put a flash thing on top of it. And I think he always did. He had this framed picture of himself from before we met. It was on the front page of a 1963 copy of the *Manhattan Heights Times* (a community newspaper that was "dedicated to informing the Negro citizens of Lubbock"). Eugene had just come back from a conference in Dallas, and in the picture he was holding his camera. The article said:

Mr. Eugene Roquemore, 1808 East 26th Street, has just returned from Dallas, Texas, where he attended the 11th Annual National Industrial Photographic Conference from July 21 through 26th. All meetings were held at the Memorial Auditorium and Adolphus Hotel. At the Adolphus Hotel Negro and White boarded during the meeting.

Delegates were represented from Little Rock, Arkansas; New Orleans, Louisiana; Orangeburge, South Carolina; New York; New Jersey; Houston, Austin, Waco, and Dallas, Texas.

Classes in picture coloring, retouching, portraits, laboratory techniques, commercial photography, and bridal weddings were given at the conference. Each photographer who attended this conference was able to carry back to their home the new and exciting methods in the field of photography.

That was a good picture of Eugene, but it was before I knew him. We met at church. He went to church, and whenever people would want a picture made, they'd ask him to make it. And if he had the time and if he wasn't on the job, he went and made the picture. So I met him at church, at the Rising Star Baptist Church.

He was working at Frito-Lay before his health started failing him. He worked on the truck, on this conveyor. The boxes would come down and he would place them on something that went into the truck. Then one time he was working at packaging the Fritos and potato chips. And then, from '76 until the time he retired in '86, he worked sanitation, I believe that's what you call it. I would say he worked at Frito for about twenty-two years. That would be my guess. They have a big Frito plant here. It's over on Avenue A and 34th, about a whole block from there.

Eugene would take pictures at the Frito-Lay picnics every year. They had an annual picnic that was usually at McKenzie Park. It would last all day; we'd go out early in the morning and stay until mid-afternoon, when we'd leave. They'd play all kind of games and have all this food stretched out there. They'd get a caterer to come out and bring the food—good old barbecue and baked beans and potato salad and all of that. They'd have this tug of war—I guess that was it, these rope pullings—and then volleyball and dominoes and cards and just a picnic. Then the kids could go and play on the rides—it was at the fair and the kids would go and ride the rides and all. It lasted all day long and it was just a good fun affair. And he made pictures galore.

He took pictures of people of all colors. Sometimes he even took pictures at white people's weddings. I know at least two or three families that worked at Frito-Lay and they asked him to make their pictures. And I know we went to this white church one time. I went with him twice to a white church to make pictures at weddings. And they were just nice like everybody else; it was real enjoyable. And, of course, they paid for film and everything and all the work that it took to make the pictures, and at that rate, whatever they gave him was profit on a wedding like that.

The photographs of Eugene's that stand out the most with me are my family pictures. He made the pictures of my mother, my grandmother and my sisters and brothers. In other words, we have five generations on his side of the family and mine. Oh, everybody just loved Eugene, I think. One thing that made them love him so was that he was a real nice kind-hearted man. He would rather do something for somebody for nothing than to ask them to pay if he felt like they couldn't. He didn't want to hurt anybody's feelings. He would do anything for anybody. He had reared some of his nieces and nephews and he supported his mother from the time he come out of service until the day she died. She lived with him. She was a widow lady

when he come from service; so he took care of her and the family, and also the friends and anybody else that he could do anything for to help them.

Eugene had been married previously before our marriage. And I asked him one day, "What happened to you in this first marriage?" I didn't know the lady he married. I remember when the lady died and I know some of her people here. He had one son, Robert Earl, and if there were any others I didn't know about it. They were married and separated and divorced in the same year that they got married. And I asked him what happened there. I said, "Well, honey, how come you didn't stay married to the lady? What happened?" And he looked at me real strange and got tickled and said, "She was too jealous." I said, "What you mean too jealous?" And then when he told me what she was jealous for, I said, "Well, I can't blame her for being jealous, if that's what you call jealous."

You see, when he come from service, he told me that his mamma and daddy had separated and divorced and his daddy was married to another lady and he was so hurt and so disappointed until he said, "Mother, I'm gonna take care of you the rest of your life." And my understanding, from what he could tell me, what the other lady was jealous about was when he went to work. Well, she already had a family and two daughters; one was in college and the other was getting ready to go to college. And when he got married, he had left his mother in the place that he was paying rent on and he continued to take care of his mother and these nieces and nephews and whoever else that was there. But he moved in with the lady that he married. And when he would go to work—this is hearsay—he would have to go by and check on his mother, and when he got off of work, before he would go home to his wife, he would stop and check on his mother. Well, that's enough to make any lady, you know, wonder. "If you are my husband, then you are going to come home." But he put mother, to make a long story short, ahead of wife, and I don't blame the lady one bit and I told him that I wouldn't have stayed with him either [under those circumstances].

During World War II Eugene was in the army. I didn't know him at that time. I just read his discharge papers and about the medals and different things that he accumulated while he

was in service. And he also brought some sou-
venirs back from service that were stolen from
us since we been out here. I couldn't tell you
what they were; all I could do is describe them.
One was what I guess you'd call a sword. It was
sharp on each side and it was his pride and joy
that he brought from overseas with him when
he come from Germany and France. He got
four bronze stars.

Well, after he got out of the service, he went
to Wiley College, where he studied photography. And he became a good photographer, and
a teacher too. He taught me to take pictures at
a birthday party once. I told him that I wanted
to make a picture of him cutting his own cake.
And he said, "Well, I'm gonna show you how."
And he took the camera, placed it in my hand,
and showed me how to hold it and how to look
through the little viewfinder. Then he said
"Hold it steady. Don't shake one way or another. And when you get a certain place where you
can see what you want to see through this
viewfinder, then you push this little button. And
when you push the little button, make sure you
hold it straight and firm so you won't get a
motion." And I did just that. But the first one I
made, it was kind of one-sided. He said, "You
didn't do what I told you to do! Come back and
hold it like I tell you and stand right here." He
positioned me where to stand at a distance
from him. And he said, "Now, you think you can
hold this camera?" And I told him, "Yes." I could
hold it. And that turned out to be the most beautiful picture that I have of him cutting his own
birthday cake.

Eugene just loved taking pictures. He'd take
pictures of anything. A lot of times he would
want to make a group of pictures and people
wouldn't be standing like he thought they
should and he'd lay the camera down and go
and stand them and turn them and tell them
how to pose. That's what I would call it—how to
get the feet straight and put the legs like they
were supposed to be and all that sort of stuff.

A lot of times he would just come in from
Frito-Lay and I know the guy would be tired, he
would spend eight hours over there. But somebody would call on the telephone and say, "Mr.
Roquemore, we're having such and such a
thing. Could you come and make a picture for
me?" And he'd be eating and he'd say, "Well...."
I'd say, "No, you can't go, honey, you can't go.

You're too tired. You can't go; you haven't had a
bath." And he'd say, "Well, let me see. What
time is it?" And he'd talk and eat and talk and
eat and before it was over with, I'd be running
bath water and getting out a camera and seeing
if he had film. He would just stop eating sometimes and get up and go make a picture of
whatever the occasion was. A lot of times
school kids would call him. And if the basketball team or the football team was going somewhere to play, he'd work overtime to be able to
get off so he could go to that game and make a
picture of somebody out there at school. And at
church sometimes he would have the money to
get all of his film and stuff like that and I'd tell
him, "We aren't gonna be able to pay bills if you
keep making pictures." And he'd just laugh at
me and say, "God will make a way. I like to
make pictures." So he'd just make a picture of
anything.

He made more pictures of churches and
groups of people than I can remember. He'd
take them down near the Civic Center and
make pictures there just for the scenery. And
sometimes with a niece or a nephew or a friend
or anybody, he'd stand them by the scenery and
make pictures. And a lot of time when it
snowed and everything, he'd just go out and
make pictures of the snow and everything like
that.

Eugene was a jack of all trades, I guess.
That's what I would call him because he loved
to go and piddle around and arrange people.
Now when we'd go down to my mother's house
during summer, he'd get out there under that
old chinaberry tree and spread out a blanket
and everybody came around and acted like they
were having a picnic. He'd pass the soda pop
around, potato chips, and all that sort of stuff.
He'd want you to look a certain way and turn a
certain way for him to get a picture. He just
loved to make pictures. But he never had his
own darkroom. He used Mr. Roberts's studio for
years and then he went to Fox Photo.

The last picture that Eugene made was of
me and my family when we were over on Park
Lane at a cousin of mine's house. There was a
group of us, he couldn't hold the camera up to
make the picture right. He was too weak. That
was in 1992 and he died a year later.

Pictures were important in the lives of the
people Eugene photographed. If it was a wed-

Unknown maker, *Eugene Rocquemore in the Army,* Henderson, Texas, ca. 1940s.

ding, that's something that you can look at for the rest of your life and enjoy. If it was a family group or a church group, it's the same way. In other words, I think, for me, I like pictures, because when I'm here by myself in the daytime, especially when my brother's not here, I might get out a box of pictures and spend the whole day looking at them and thinking about when this happened and what the occasion was. It's something that you can have and keep—to see when a child was small; now she's a grown lady, has her own children, and all of that. It's fascinating to me that you can put something on a paper that you can look at when you can't look at the person.

In 1993, Eric Strong [from Texas Tech University] put together an exhibit of some of Eugene's photographs. And one day there was a group of TV people going to come by to see it with some newspaper people, and they wanted to interview Eugene. I remember saying, "No, you don't need to go because you're tired and your health is not that good." But he went anyway; he decided to go ahead and go to the interview, and in my opinion it seemed to make him feel good. So that made me feel good. Well, I went to the grocery store and I told Eric to come pick him up. But when he came back and

told me he had this interview and he was down there and he was doing all of this, my conscience bothered me. I was so glad that Eric did come get him. I didn't know that exhibit was that important to him. I said, "Eric, if I had known you was really going to come and take him, I would have missed going to the grocery store to go with him down there myself."

Well, when he was taking pictures, it was never really appreciated the way that it should have been. People didn't realize the value of his work and what he was doing. But he thought that it was important for people to know that he had a collection of photographs and that they were available. You'd come by and he could find whatever you were looking for. I don't know what kind of filing system he had, but he could just about get to whatever he wanted to get to.

In other words, the filing system he had was in his head. He had all of his photographs in boxes. He had them laying here, there, anywhere. Oh, he had them in his car; he had them in my car. If he made a picture last week and he went up there and developed it and made a picture, he'd bring it and show it to me and then he'd put it in the car. He might see you down the street and he'd show it to you, and if you paid him for it, he'd take the money. It was just something that he wanted to do and he would rather do that than go do something that I thought was important.

He felt like he was pleasing people and pleasing himself too, because he liked to make pictures. He would rather make pictures than to just go out on an outing. In other words, I asked him a lot of times, "Why don't we go visiting? Why don't we go and do such and such thing?" And he'd say, "Well, Miss Wilson asked me to come by the church and make a picture for her group. They are going to have a, what is this they have at the school or maybe it was a debutante ball or it was Miss Black Lubbock. They were going to have the Queen Coronation. So and so asked me to come make a picture for that." And he would go, and instead of making a picture for just the ones that asked him to come, he would make a picture of everything that was happening there. Then he would go back and sell those pictures

I remember one in night in 1970. Somebody called and said, "Uncle Gene, would you come over and make a picture of us tonight?" And he asked me to go with him, and I said, "Yes, I'll go with you." My husband had died back in '68, '67, and Mr. Roquemore was such a nice man at church. Well, we went to the school fair, and when he got there with that camera, I sat there on that seat by myself and he took a picture of everybody that was participating. And then even after that, they had a social, the dance after that deal, and he went to that and he brought me home about one o'clock in the morning. So I thought, I'm not going with this man any place any more. He didn't know how to come home when he had that camera. But he invited me to go to a football game with him, and there was something about Mr. Roquemore—he was so kind and so nice—I really enjoyed going out with him. And that's the way we met, and he proposed marriage after a year or two. But anyway, I would go to ball games with him. And instead of me sitting down he'd bring me somebody to talk to and to enjoy the game with, and he'd grab his camera and he'd be way down across the field there. And if somebody made a touchdown, he'd snap that—anything. Maybe his favorite thing was doing the activities of school children, I don't know.

He'd spend all his money for film and if the person didn't offer to pay him for the film, he never asked him for it. No, he didn't get anything for a lot of the pictures, and I guess that was why he would make more than just what he was asked to do. So maybe he could get enough money out there to pay for his film and when he got so he couldn't go and develop them, he had to have that done by someone else, but he never stopped making pictures. He made them pictures until he couldn't hold that camera straight.

Eric Strong

I remember Mr. Roquemore coming to the schools. To me, he always struck me as being very professional. We had a talent show. He came out, this was in the '80s, '85–'86. He'd come out and take pictures. And I guess he had done it for a long time and he called me by here one day, and he said "I have some of the pictures from the talent show." He had really good pictures of a lot of people. And he was able to sell a lot of those pictures to the people who were in the talent show and I can remember him being at the football games and the basketball games. He seemed like the kind of person who was always there with his camera.

I was born on June 5, 1952, and I had a real happy childhood in Lubbock. I lived down the street from the Roquemores when I was growing up and had the opportunity to go by the house on occasion. I remember some of the social unrest. A lot of it I don't remember. One night there was a lady who they were going to evict from her home and a lot of people decided that it wasn't fair. And there was a little bit of unrest with that.

When I was growing up, I didn't realize the importance of what Mr. Roquemore was doing. He was a guy who was just there with the pictures. He got the baseball team together and said, "You sit here; you move around here." And he stood and took the pictures and he would sell those pictures to you. He had done it for so long that he knew what to say and how to say it and to make sure that he followed through on that—I thought he was very good at what he did.

Eugene Roquemore, *Street Scene*, Henderson, Texas, ca. 1940s.

Eugene Roquemore, *Roquemore's Studio*, Henderson, Texas, ca. 1950.

Eugene Roquemore, *Mrs. Roquemore (Eugene Roquemore's mother)*, Henderson, Texas, ca. 1950.

Eugene Roquemore, *Couple*, Lubbock, Texas, ca. 1950s.

Eugene Roquemore, *Coronation*, Lubbock, Texas, ca. 1960s.

Eugene Roquemore, *Parade*, Lubbock, Texas, ca. 1950s.

Eugene Roquemore, *Couple Dancing at the Cotton Club*, Lubbock, Texas, ca. 1950s.

Eugene Roquemore, *Group Scene at the Cotton Club,* Lubbock, Texas, ca. 1950s.

Eugene Roquemore, *Pony Ride*, Lubbock, Texas, ca. 1950s.

Eugene Roquemore, *Self-Portrait*, Lubbock, Texas, ca. 1950s.

Eugene Roquemore, *Barber Shop*, Lubbock, Texas, ca. 1960s.

Eugene Roquemore, *Parade,* Lubbock, Texas, ca. 1960s.

Eugene Roquemore, *Drum Major and Majorettes,* Lubbock, Texas, ca. 1960s.

Eugene Roquemore, *High School Graduate*, Lubbock, Texas, ca. 1960s.

Eugene Roquemore, *Two Women at the Cotton Club*, Lubbock, Texas, ca. 1960s.

152

Eugene Roquemore, *Backyard Football*, Lubbock, Texas, ca. 1960s.

Eugene Roquemore, *Seated Couples,* Lubbock, Texas, ca. 1960s.

Eugene Roquemore, *Wedding Couple,* Lubbock, Texas, ca. 1960s.

Ivery Myers

I've spent most of my time in life getting an education. I was born on May 2, 1919, the son of Abram and Charlotte Myers, near Bay City, Texas. I left there when I was about fourteen and I attended several schools. The first was Prairie View College, where I received a bachelor's degree. Then I went to Texas Southern University in Houston for a master's degree, and later on I went to the University of Texas to study on a Ph.D. in higher education.

My bachelor's was in business administration with a minor in social sciences. At Texas Southern, I got a master's in education. And then, when I went to the University of Texas, I had an idea to further my studies in higher education, meaning, of course, on the college level up in universities. I never finished my Ph.D. because I had begun to have children. And I had to stay in Houston and take care of them and educate them.

I taught at a rural high school in Travis County, Texas. And I was the principal of a grade one through twelve school at the age of twenty-four. Then from there, I went into the photography business, inspired by Arthur Chester Teal.

I learned about photography from Teal while I was in Prairie View working on my bachelor's. Mr. Teal came to Prairie View in 1943 or '42. He was looking for a place to establish a little branch office at the Prairie View campus because most of his jobs kept him too busy to adequately serve Prairie View and all their activities and things of that sort. So he let me be his salesman and representative at Prairie View. I was recommended by the dean of men, Mr. Hilliard, to be the right man to help open Mr. Teal's studio there.

The first day he gave me a briefcase of sam- ples, a receipt book, and offered me 25 percent commission on all orders sold by the time he came to Houston to shoot the pictures. That first day in a matter of two and half hours, I had earned eighty-nine dollars, which was very exciting to me. I vowed that first day that I was going to make photography my avocation. I made enough money on that campus selling for Mr. Teal to pay my tuition, buy my clothes, and every other thing that I wanted.

Mr. Teal was a businessman. He was a friendly man. I never saw him meet a person that he didn't become friends with. Mr. Teal was the son of a tinsmith out of Crockett, Texas. He said his father taught him how to treat the public, even though his father was not a pho- tographer.

I don't think Mr. Teal made tintypes, though he did help his father around a little bit. I don't know where he got his photography education. When I met him he was very near fifty years old.

And after I graduated from Prairie View, I managed Mr. Teal's studio in San Antonio, Texas, at 1066 Sycamore Street, which was next door to the USO in 1944–1945. I worked for Teal's studio for one year and did more sales managing than photography work, though I did learn photography in his darkroom while I was there. I didn't go to his formal school of pho- tography at all.

I think Teal only kept the studio in San Antonio for four or five years during World War II. His studio in Houston was the main office, and he possibly also worked in Dallas and in his hometown of Crockett. His wife, Elnora, was a photographer too, and she was operating her own studio. Mrs. Teal operated her person- al studio at their home on Breckinridge Street,

I believe. Mr. Teal had his studio at 2213½ Dowling Street, right in the heart of the Third Ward.

Mr. Teal was a great salesman. He had a very good knack for making sales. I learned a lot from him in making sales. If a customer would come in, Mr. Teal would first talk to them about the time of the day, you know, that type of thing. But he would gradually go back to the subject at hand. He did not let the prospective customer go away without making a sitting for him. He would find something attractive about that subject, and he might not even shoot those pictures the same day you come in. He established a cohesiveness with that customer that the customer might come back that same day and wear a certain color or a certain kind of clothing to make that picture in. He was very good on making his sales. You might come in there for one picture, but after having made a ten-dollar deposit for one picture, he might sell you at least sixty or seventy dollars' worth of pictures before you left that place.

Teal was also very much of an artist. Teal taught the help that he hired. He was a man who would go out and train his people, except for one Japanese photographer that came there. His name was Fakuda, and he had worked for Teal for several years. But in 1942 Fakuda was sent to a "concentration" camp, where they sent most American Japanese. I don't know if he was a full citizen of America or not.

Well, one day Fakuda was walking around San Antonio while I was working there. He saw the name of the Teal studio from the street and he walked in the door. He had gotten out of the "concentration" camp, and he said, "Is this the Mr. Teal headquartered in Houston?"

I said, "Yes, come on in." And he walked in the door. And he sat down and told me his story. So I immediately got on the telephone and called Mr. Teal in Houston at his headquarters there.

He said, "Mr. Myers, don't let that man leave your studio. If it's necessary, let him sleep there all night." So I kept Fakuda there. Fakuda was a very good darkroom man. He was a big help. Elnora Frazier and Arthur Williams worked with me in San Antonio. I did the sales, and they did the darkroom work. But on that day they were out for lunch. And I had these customers come in, a whole group of singers.

Unknown maker, *A. C. Teal*, Houston, Texas, ca. 1941.

Mr. Fakuda said, "Mr. Myers, I shoot the picture for you." And he took his camera out, a 4x5, and started taking the pictures. But his language, of course, his vocabulary was very limited. He was trying to get the attention of one of them, and said, "the woman there." And the lady said, "Who, me?"

He said, "No, the black one." Well, I almost lost that sale. That woman cursed me out and cursed Fakuda out.

She said, "That's why they had the Japanese there in the concentration camp. They ought to send you back over there."

At that time, the word "black" was out. They used the word "Negro." And people in that line had different shades of colors. So he said "that black one."

He said, "Mr. Myers, what did I do? Why did

that woman curse at me?" And I had to call him back in the office and explain to him, but I had an hour explanation to do to that woman who brought that group of singers there.

Mr. Teal photographed everybody, white people too. Of course, until the civil rights laws were passed, black people could not go to white studios and make their pictures. Teal had all the towns in Texas. He was brilliant. He had all kinds of people working for him. He had the Cantus; they did art work, tinting, retouching. The Cantus were a family that lived in Houston. They were very loyal to Mr. Teal.

Mr. Teal was the first photographer I know that made a contribution of $11,000 when Texas Southern University was getting started in the 1940s. He made a gift as a philanthropist. Teal had a wonderful attitude about himself and about meeting people. He was very businesslike until he decided on the weekends he wanted to go out. He liked to eat fine foods.

Mr. Teal was about five feet six or less and he looked to weigh about 150–160 pounds. He had light skin. He wore a goatee all the time and he was an immaculate dresser. He always dressed formally. I never saw him in general work clothes. He was always in his studio that he operated there on Dowling, and he greeted the people at the door when his receptionist was there and when she wasn't there. Teal served as an inspiration to many people. He made the economics of those persons who he knew gratifying because he was quite interested in helping people in school. I know that he helped me through school.

I'm glad to have had the chance to work with Mr. Teal, and to have been the manager of his studio in San Antonio. That was a very popular studio. After I left Teal, I went back to the school business. But I continued photography as my avocation. Mr. Teal prepared me to be able to work as a journalist. I also taught journalism in the high schools of Houston and New Orleans. I started at Booker T. Washington High, and then from there I went to Abraham Lincoln, Jack Yates High School, you name it. I worked at several high schools in this city.

In 1945–46 I was managing editor of the New Orleans *Sentinel.* I moved there after I left Teal. I taught high school in New Orleans and one summer at Dillard University. And I made pictures of movie stars during the Texas City disaster, when I was living in New Orleans. They came there for a benefit show: Frank Sinatra, Jack Benny, and a big show group came to New Orleans.

I also made pictures of Louis Armstrong, who was Zulu King for the Mardi Gras. I think that was 1945, and he came down the Mississippi singing "Basin Street" and "Sleepy Time Down South." I had a wonderful collection. All the negatives I brought back to Houston with me when I left there. I stayed in New Orleans and worked there from 1945 to 1950, when I came to Houston to take a job at Texas Southern University.

I was assistant administrator in business at Texas Southern. And around that time my collection got destroyed. I had my wardrobe trunk with all those negatives in there. And when I came back to Houston to live again, I brought those negatives with me in 4x5 boxes. One day, we were cleaning up or something and they got thrown in the trash. I had a wonderful collection.

A. C. Teal, *Teal School of Photography*, Houston, Texas, ca. 1947.

Teal Studio, *C. W. Hicks Sr.,* Houston, Texas, 1927. *Courtesy Houston Metropolitan Research Center.*

Teal Studio, *John Fletcher, Waiter on the Southern Pacific Railroad,* Houston, Texas, ca. 1920s. *Courtesy Houston Metropolitan Research Center.*

Teal Studio, *Cora Toliver Washington, Seamstress,* Houston, Texas, ca. 1920s. *Courtesy Houston Metropolitan Research Center.*

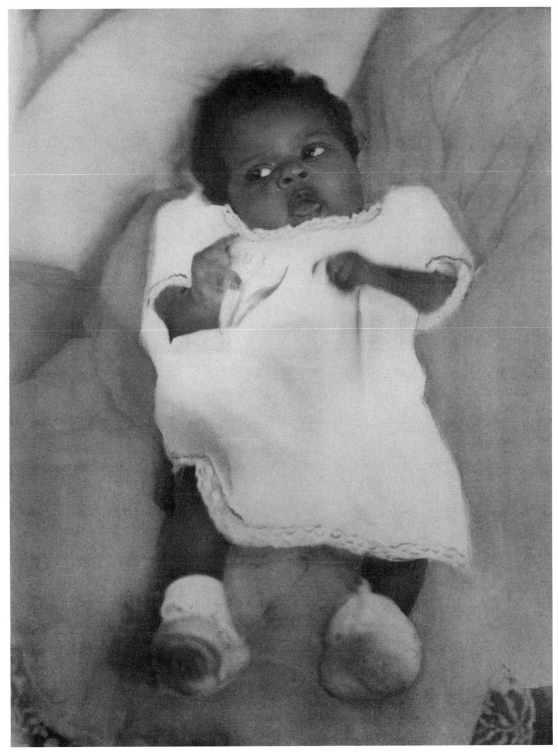

Teal Studio, *Bettye L. Hicks*, Houston, Texas, 1930. *Courtesy Houston Metropolitan Research Center.*

Unknown maker, *A. C. Teal (left), J. H. Jemison Sr. (right)*, Houston, Texas, ca. 1940s. *Courtesy Houston Metropolitan Research Center.*

A. C. Teal, *Graduation Portrait of S. E. Palmer, Prairie View State College*, Prairie View, Texas, 1931.

164

A. C. Teal, *Senior Class of Prairie View State College*, Prairie View, Texas, 1931.

A. C. Teal, *Wedding*, Houston, Texas, ca. 1940s. Courtesy Ivery Myers.

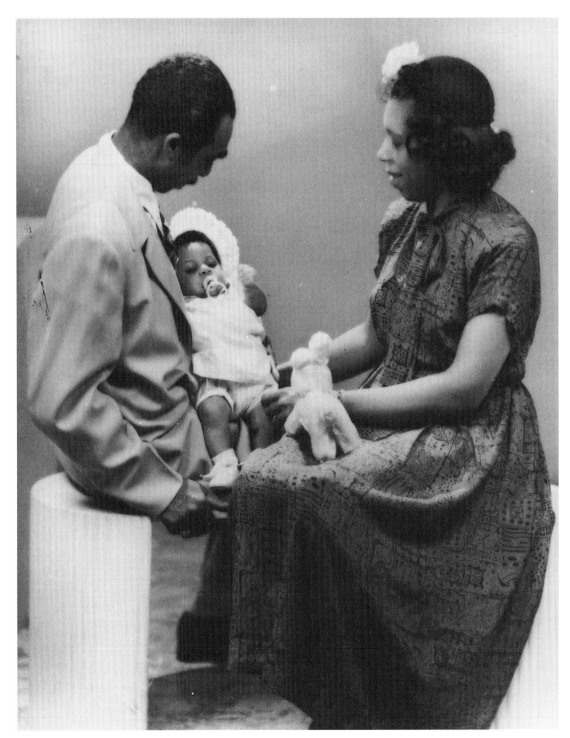

A. C. Teal, *Marshall, Marsha, and Elnora Frazier,* Houston, Texas, 1950.

A. C. Teal, *Elnora Frazier*, Houston, Texas, 1950.
Hand-tinted gelatin silver print.

A. C. Teal, *Elnora Frazier and her daughter Marsha*,
Houston, Texas, 1951.

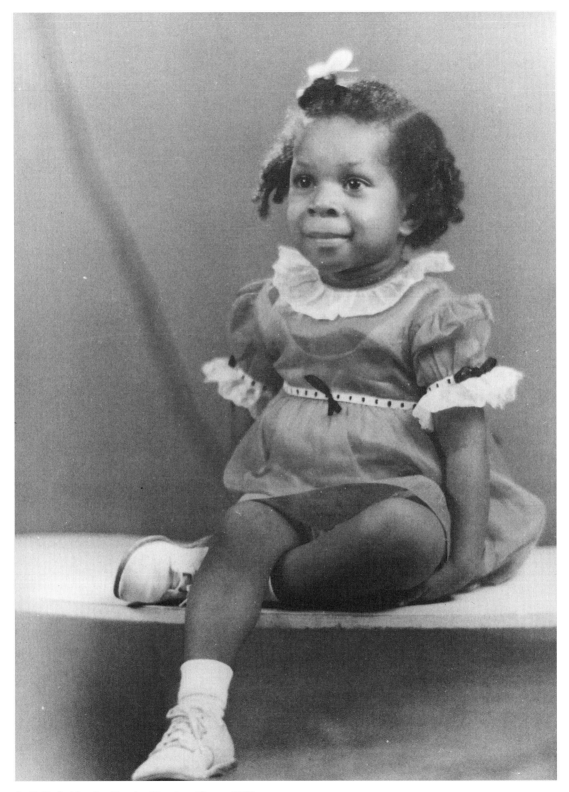

A. C. Teal, *Marsha Frazier,* Houston, Texas, 1952.

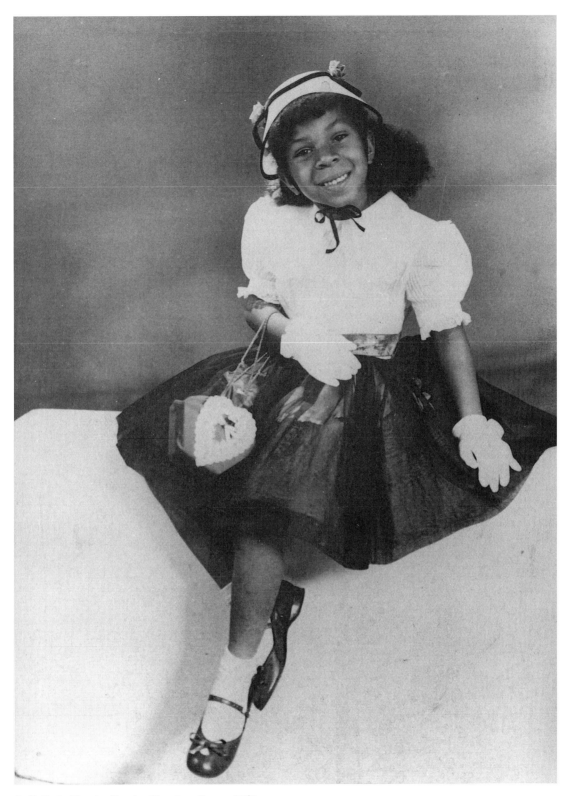

A. C. Teal, *Marsha Frazier*, Houston, Texas, 1954.

Elnora Frazier

I was the oldest in my family. I was born on January 10, 1924, in Fifth Ward, and later we moved to Second Ward. That was at an early age. And when I really began to know about things, we moved to Third Ward.

I attended Douglass Elementary School and then Jack Yates High School. I graduated in 1940 and went to Houston College. At that time it was called Houston Negro College.

I became interested in photography after I graduated from high school because Mr. Teal, who was a noted black photographer at the time, advertised that he was going to have classes. And I saw the advertisement and I became real interested. He had the classes in his studio. They were held at night in Third Ward on Dowling Street. It was above the Dowling Theater.

He had a nice studio with a waiting room, photographic room, printing room, and his office. Mr. Teal was a very interesting man. He wanted you to be the best, and I think he portrayed that through his teachings, because there were a number of his students who came out and went into photography professionally. He was a good person to work for as far as I was concerned. He treated me as a lady, and I worked as one of his all-around employees after I graduated from his school. He had the classes in 1942. I was in his first graduating class. Juanita Williams was in that class too. That's when we became friends.

Mr. Teal hadn't taken any family pictures of me when I was younger. I became acquainted with him when I first started his classes and met him. At the time he was the only black photographer who could get the jobs in the black schools. So each year he would be at the schools taking pictures of the graduates and photographs of anything else that was special

going on at the schools. And of course he was quite well known through all of that.

Mr. Teal's classes were at night and I think the first class lasted from six to nine months. Each session was three hours, and went three nights a week. And after about nine months he gave us a certificate.

Mr. Teal's wife, Elnora, was also a photographer. She had her own business in her home. And Mr. Teal had his business established in the place that he had rented. They lived in the Fifth Ward. I was mostly associated with Mr. Teal. Juanita Williams was mostly associated with Mrs. Teal. She kind of grew up with them.

When I first started working for Mr. Teal, I did things in the darkroom: loading film holders, developing the film, and also mixing the chemicals. In those days, he did a lot of work and you would buy your chemicals in fifty-gallon cartons or containers and make your own developer and fixing bath. So I did that. That's how I first started off. And later I became a printer, then naturally I became a receptionist. And I assisted him in photographs. I was an assistant and helped arrange lights and film and things of that sort.

He had someone else working on the hand-coloring. Mr. Teal photographed it, but it was Mr. Cantu that tinted it. And he had somebody do his retouching. His name was Mr. Fakuda. He was Japanese.

Mr. Cantu did great coloring, and Mr. Fakuda was put in a detention camp during the war because he was Japanese. Mr. Teal began his advanced class in photography when the veterans were coming back from the war. The government was paying for anything the fellows wanted to do to complete their schooling. Those advanced classes were not the ones I attended, but the classes that he later held when there wasn't any school of photography in any colleges that blacks could attend in the city of Houston. So Teal founded his school out of the need, and maybe two or three years later they established Texas Southern University. Jack Yates School was used in the daytime for high school students and used at night as a college. Mr. Teal turned an old house at the corner of Live Oak and Holman into a lab, because he couldn't have it in the studio.

Hiram Dotson was one of Mr. Teal's students and he later became the photographer for the *Forward Times.* And he also became an engraver. He's with the *Forward Times* of today. There are two other women photographers I remember. I think they're now deceased. T. Bertha Williams ran a studio in the Third Ward. She attended my church and that's why I still have strong memories of her. And there was also another lady who was good. Her name was Edna Tarver and she also worked for Mr. Teal. She was affiliated with the church quite a bit, because she even took pictures of the pastor.

I helped Louise Martin a couple of times when she was in the school season. She was kind of rushed. I worked with her maybe three or four times.

I worked for Mr. Teal for about fifteen years. He died in 1956. I continued to work for Mrs. Teal off and on, but it wasn't on a regular basis. I obtained another job. I did black-and-white finishing at Courtesy Photo Supply. And I waited on customers. The owner had a little camera shop, and I waited on customers when his wife went out to deliver her routes. At that time her routes mostly consisted of drug stores.

Around 1982 I went to work for NPL [National Photographic Labs] as a printer. I worked there for about seven years, and then I retired in 1989. During those years I also more or less worked for myself. I would only do pictures off and on for friends and relatives because I've always been affiliated with some form of studio as a daily worker.

I've done a few groups at my church, the Fourth Missionary Baptist Church. I made the choir pictures a couple of times. But, as I said I didn't do much outside work because I was always already working every day. And I've been married forty-six years to my husband, Marshall. My maiden name is Williams. And we

have one daughter, Marsha Frazier. I took a lot of pictures of her while she was growing up. She's about forty-three now.

My first cameras were little, the Brownie Hawkeye and whatnot, and after that I got into the 4x5 camera. I got a Speed Graphic. Later I used a Mimaya. Mr. Teal used an 8x10 camera, and also 5x7 and 4x5. The only time I used the larger format was when I did some photographing and working in his studio.

The only way you could become a good printer was to learn about shading, burning, and dodging. I used lenses that would fit over certain enlargers that could give different diffusing effects, and different filters, too. They have different filters that give different effects. I used to have a darkroom of my own.

I did my own oils. Tinting was what they called it at the time. I used Marshall oils, but my tinting was confined to things I did for myself. I never did any outside tinting for anybody. I like the Kodak fiber paper. The Koda-bromide was fashionable at that time. In the 1960s I became acquainted with the RC paper when I was working for Floyd Photo doing photo finishing. They serviced drug stores and any professional photographers that would come in and want finished work. I worked there about ten years.

I've always been interested in painting and drawing. I took a little recreation night course at the Houston Community College, probably in the 1980s. And I've started at it again. Oh, I've always been interested.

I made one drawing in 1991 or 1992 that was of me at an early age, as a young mother, maybe. It's imaginary. It's as if going in the garden in the morning was the rendition of the feeling, because you can get so much inspiration from going into the garden and getting all your thoughts from daily happenings. It's sort of like meeting God there, because you see the things of nature. You look and you see how the corn is growing when actually it only came from a seed, a little small seed. And you see the cabbage and you can watch the development from day to day. And you can even see some of the little bad things, such as the worms that might eat on the cabbage. And the garden is such an inspiration because you can watch the flowers. It just sort of takes your mind away from anything that might come up on that day or on another day. Perhaps it's things you

Dottie Walker, *Elnora Frazier at Work at NPL Labs,* Houston, Texas, 1988.

thought about before you went to the garden. That's the way I view that. Fresh air.

You could say that my drawing and painting are like my photography in the way I put a little of me in it. Even in photographing, you always want to put a little of you, a little of your individuality in anything that you do. That's what separates you from the next person, even though the next person might be better at something than you. But it's your own interpretation, the way you see it and the way you feel it. That's why some people can get better photographs than others. It's not just a matter of sitting a person before a camera. You have to be able to get something from that person. They have some personality or whatnot that they can radiate through that picture that you're either drawing or photographing.

It comes from a vision. Vision, you might say, is in a different plane. It's just not an ordinary thing. I think it's extraordinary. In the manner that I use "vision," sometimes it's something that you don't really know until it happens. Even in speaking or in anything that you do, it's like something that just comes, sort of like a gift.

When I'm making something, I feel that way. There are times when I start a painting and I don't know where it's going to end. The drawing of me in the garden probably took a couple of months, because I only would do fine detailing on it when I had an inspiration. At first I didn't know whether I wanted to have the mountain or how I wanted the trees to look. I did know that I wanted a big sunflower. I like the sunflower because it reminds me of a birth of a new day; how it opens, how it portrays itself. That to me is the inspiration of the morning. It's new each morning. That's the way life can be. Each day is a new day and is a different day and it's what you put into it that will make it appear the way you see it.

Elnora Frazier, *Elaine Williams (Elnora Frazier's niece)*, Houston, Texas, ca. 1960s.

Elnora Frazier, *Alice Jones,* Houston, Texas, ca. 1960s.

Elnora Frazier, *Clara Everline*, Houston, Texas, ca. 1960s.

Elnora Frazier, *Standing Woman,* Houston, Texas, ca. 1960s.

Elnora Frazier, *Twirler*, Houston, Texas, ca. 1960s.

Elnora Frazier, *Marsha Frazier*, Houston, Texas, ca. 1966. *Hand-tinted gelatin silver print.*

Elnora Frazier, *Portrait,* Houston, Texas, ca. 1970s.

Juanita Williams

My parents worked on the farm near Stafford, Texas. Their names were Lucy and Johnny Williams. I was born on November 16, 1926, and my father died when I was four years old. We stayed with my grandparents in Stafford until I was six and my mother moved to Houston, to the Fifth Ward. I had six sisters and three brothers, and while I was still in school my sister Helen got an apartment from the Teals. They lived at 2218 Breckenridge, and my sister's apartment was near their house. They had apartments right behind them and down the street.

My sister would work late and she'd ask me to go over to Mrs. Teal's. And I'd go over there and then I would watch her, you know, as she was doing things. I observed her and that's how I really began with it, because her husband was going out of town a lot. He'd take pictures of different schools, small schools, and he'd be on the road a lot. So she was glad for me to spend time with her. I would just watch her, and then finally I just got interested and she taught me.

Mr. Teal had a school for photography at his studio in the Third Ward. It was upstairs above the Dowling Theater on Dowling Street. Mrs. Teal ran the studio in the Fifth Ward, and he worked in the Third Ward.

I started working with Mrs. Teal in 1941 and 1942. I made up the chemicals, and then she taught me how to use the printer. So I would go in and print, and later I learned how to retouch. I learned how to put the orders together and wait on the customers. Then finally Mr. Teal started a class in an art gallery and I learned how to hand-color photographs. But they couldn't find hardly anybody to do any retouching. He did have a Japanese man before the war, but when the war came, the Japanese man had to go to one of those [detention] camps. So I started helping Mr. Teal with the retouching.

I finished the Teal School in 1944. So he must have started at the end of 1942, the beginning of 1943. He wanted me to be an instructor over at Texas Southern [University] but at the time, after I became a mother I really didn't particularly want anything to do with photography. But I kept on and kept on and just kept learning more and more about it. Then, I started working for another lady. Her last name was Bradley. I've forgotten her first name, but I did retouching for her. She was up there near Sears on Main Street. She was a white photographer, but she went out to California soon after I started with her.

I worked for Teal for about ten years, from about 1941 to 1951. Then I went to work for Mrs. Bradley, and after she went to California I left for Seattle in 1952. I got a job doing photofinishing. I stayed there for a while and then moved back to Houston. That's when I met Herbert Provost and Benny Joseph. Benny Joseph was working at the VA Hospital and did his photography during his time off. But he started liking it and he just went on and went into business for himself. Benny also studied with Teal. Teal's classes were at night because he had the studio in the daytime. Some of the classes were at his studio and others he started at TSU [Texas Southern University].

A lot of times Mr. Teal wouldn't be available to take pictures, but his wife would not go out and make any pictures. She would get me to always go and take the pictures of the groups or whatever the people would call for. Mrs. Teal only took the photographs in the studio. And the photographs themselves were never signed, but were stamped with the name of the Teal studio, regardless of who took the pictures.

Mr. Teal was always busy and on the go, and

he traveled a lot all over Texas. And he did work for Prairie View. And for my last two or three years working with him, I was the one he would send up to do the pictures for Prairie View. He might have had six or seven people working for him. He really was a good photographer. He started just about everybody. That's why he began his school. Mrs. Teal even gave her sister in Waco some training in it.

There really weren't that many black photographers around during that time. There were the ones Teal taught, and there was Louise Martin. I really didn't work with Louise. I went and helped her. She got into a tight jam one time, and she didn't know how to print her negatives. She was afraid that she didn't have time to go back and photograph the students at Booker T. Washington. I think that was her first year that she had done Booker T. Washington School, and she got into a jam and so I went and showed her how to get out of the jam.

I was married in 1945 and my son, Craig Ronald Miller, was born a year later. Right now, he's a shoe manager in a K-Mart store. I took a lot of pictures of him when he was growing up. My husband and I separated in the 1950s. He died in 1975.

I went to Phyllis Wheatley High School, and I also took up courses in being a nursing assistant. And I got my license in underwriting life insurance. I wrote for the National Western Life Insurance company for two years.

I did a lot of work for Mr. C. P. Clay, who had a Baptist seminary in Alabama. I did all his pictures whenever he would come to Houston to give different people their degrees for studying with him. And in 1965 he gave me one in business for all the work I did. He sent for me to come to Birmingham, and he felt I should get something for what I had done.

I've done a lot of different kinds of work, but mostly I've done photo-finishing. I worked for Mr. and Mrs. Bartha at Courtesy Photo from 1954 until I built this house in 1962 in the east Sunnyside neighborhood. I moved back to Houston from Seattle because my mother was ill and I wanted to see about her. And I just stayed, and I had my own studio. I worked with different friends and of course after my church found out that I did pictures, well, I did pictures

Elnora Frazier, *Juanita Williams at Courtesy Photo Lab*, Houston, Texas, ca. 1960.

for my church. That's the Tabernacle Baptist Church. I took pictures of Sunday school graduations, picnics, artwork, and just different things. Some people wanted me to take pictures in their homes.

After I built this house, I decided I would go on and open up for business right here. I had a sitting room and I had a blind in the front where it wouldn't look like a house. I had a sign on there and then I had a picture window out there where they could see that I made pictures inside. I used a 4x5 camera, mostly Speed Graphic and a Crown Graphic, and I did different kinds of prints. I did a lot of sepia prints, and I used to hand-color pictures with oils. I didn't really color that much. I just put in some highlights.

And they still want me to do it. I have a Yashica D camera now. I have a lady now who wants black-and-white pictures made. She said she wants something real good for her to put on her death program. I haven't called her yet because I don't know. I just don't have my mind on it. I just do it when I feel like it. I started with it 1942, and I'm still doing it now. That makes more than fifty years.

182

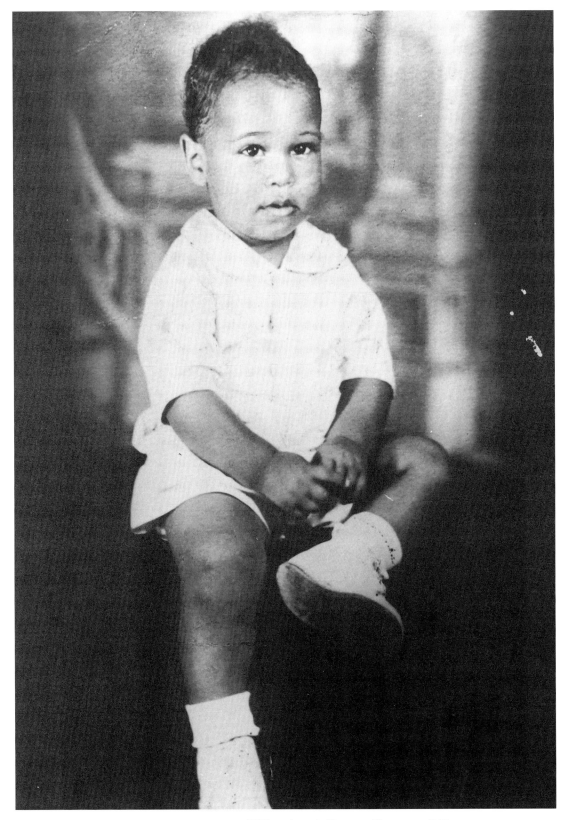

Juanita Williams, *Craig Ronald Miller (Juanita Williams's son)*, Houston, Texas, ca. 1948.

Juanita Williams, *Charles Johnson, Sylvester Johnson, Craig Ronald Miller,* Houston, Texas, ca. 1950s.

Juanita Williams, *Craig Ronald Miller*, Houston, Texas, ca. 1950s.

Juanita Williams, *Sunnyside Volunteer Fire Department,* Houston, Texas, ca. 1950s.

Elnora Frazier, *Juanita Williams*, Houston, Texas, ca. 1959.

Juanita Williams, *Lodge Group,* Houston, Texas, ca. 1960s.

Juanita Williams, *Pastor A. A. McCardell and Family,* Houston, Texas, ca. 1960s.

Juanita Williams, *Craig Ronald Miller*, Houston, Texas, ca. 1965.

Unknown maker, *Juanita Williams (fourth from left), Commencement, Union Baptist Seminary, Dr. Collier P. Clay, President,* Birmingham, Alabama, 1966.

Juanita Williams, *Lois Smith*, Houston, Texas, ca. 1970.
Hand-tinted gelatin silver print.

Juanita Williams, *Craig Ronald Miller*, Houston,
Texas, ca. 1960s. *Sepia-toned gelatin silver print.*

Benny Joseph

I've been intrigued by photography since high school when I had a friend who used to develop film. I never did learn anything from him, but he stirred my interest. I went to Blackshear Elementary School and then to Yates Junior High and High School from seventh to eleventh grades. I was in the Army from September 1943 to 1945. I served overseas, England and France.

I was born on December 10, 1924, in Lake Charles, Louisiana, but we moved to Houston after my father died. I don't know too much about my father. And I never knew my mother to have a picture taken in a studio. People just never had any money to have a photograph made in those days. My first camera was a used Speed Graphic in 1951, I think. Before that I was using more or less the school camera until I left school in '48. So, when I got home from the Army I decided to go to school on the G.I. Bill. I was in the Army from 1943 to 1945, and I went to Teal's School of Photography from 1946 to 1947.

Teal had a school for photography in connection with Houston Negro Junior College and I signed up for that. I even built my own darkroom in my garage at home and this put me ahead of my class. Houston College was a junior college, but then they started Texas State University for Negroes. Houston College was under the administration of the University of Houston, and they put in a photography department, but they didn't have any black professors. So we were brought over there at night to be taught. When the state took it over, that ended that program.

At that time Teal was the major black photographer in the state of Texas. Teal did mainly portraits. We had some snap-shooters around town, like Sid Thompson, but Teal did work all over Texas. He did all the black schools. He was known all over Texas. He knew what to do with pictures. He did good retouching. So many of the photographers coming up now don't know anything about retouching. All they do is shoot it and print it just as it comes up.

When I started out my primary interest was to do portrait photography. Of course, I had to do it all to survive. That was the main reason I went into the studio business. I wanted to do portraits. You can do it when you do school pictures, but you don't put into it like you would with a sitting coming to your studio.

There just weren't that many photographers around, and when they needed some pictures, they'd look for a commercial photographer. I was just one that people chose. I used to do a lot of things for Don Robey. He used to go hunting and he'd come back with a bunch of deer tied over his car and trailer. And they would call me to come out and take pictures of them. I did those kinds of things for Robey.

On his job promotions he would call me to take pictures of the different dances and entertainers. One of his protegés, I guess you would call him that, Robert (Bob) Garner, used to handle it for him. He's dead now.

I took one picture of Don Robey pretending to eat his hat. He made a promise to somebody that I vaguely remember. He said, "If the Bobby Bland song 'Further Up the Road' doesn't become a hit, I'll eat my hat." He decided to live up to it in a photograph, and use it for promotion. Evelyn Johnson called me to come take a shot of it.

I don't know that I ever photographed them actually recording, but he'd call me over to his studio, and he'd send them over to my studio. A lot of artists need pictures and he'd refer them to me. I took pictures of a lot of musicians. Somebody engaged me once to take photographs of B. B. King at the City Auditorium. It's torn down now. It used to sit on the corner where Jones Hall is now.

I did all kinds of photography. I photographed a guy in the north part of Houston called Houston Heights. They hung him up in a tree and scratched KKK on his chest. His name was Felton Turner. That was during the time when civil rights was in motion and Carter Wesley, the publisher of the Houston *Informer,* sent me out to take pictures of this fellow, not hanging, but after he got home. He was out of the tree, and I went to his house and took some shots. And he had KKK carved on his chest. I think they burned it on there with something, probably still on there, if he's still living. He should be, if nothing happened; he was a young man then.

I charged my normal fee. I never knew how to charge for publications or stuff like that. But when I looked up about a month later, all of these pictures were spread out in *Life* magazine. Carter Wesley sent the pictures. Of course, I didn't have no credit or anything. I didn't get paid nothing more than the ten dollars I charged him to go out and take them all. He made a killing on that, I imagine.

I did several photographs for the NAACP. I remember that they had a cafeteria for the police personnel only and some blacks were complaining that they couldn't eat in the cafeteria. During this time they had a bunch of sit-ins in jail down there and one of the civil rights bosses had me take a picture one day of them all coming out of jail. They were going to let them out at a specific time. So I was down there with my camera waiting and they had a little carnival outside and I saw a lot of the people. The public was going to the cafeteria to eat. I said, "I'm going to take a picture of this because they said it was for the police personnel only." So I threw the door open and flashed a flash with my Speed Graphic and quietly walked away. So the proprietor came by and said, "Who took that picture?" I had my camera sitting somewhere. I didn't make it known that I had taken the picture. He never did find out. I think he was kind of nervous, too, and he went back

in the cafeteria. So when the sit-ins came out, he came out with a bunch of hamburger steaks and fed all the civil rights sit-ins. I imagine that was somewhere in 1962 or '63.

I photographed them marching down the street, sitting in these different cafeterias, people getting let out of jail. The lawyers for civil rights had me taking these pictures for their records. What they did with them I don't know. I don't think I still have any of those pictures. I can't find them. I looked for them already. Evidently I don't have them filed under civil rights, or that group that was called PYA, Progressive Youth Association. I don't have them filed under that name, or their leader's name, Stearns. I've looked under the lawyers' names. There were Francis Williams, George Washington and others, but those negatives weren't there. They must have gotten those negatives.

I remember one time I wanted to take some night pictures downtown. I set up my camera on Main Street and I was taking a time shot when an officer walked up. He asked, "What have you done?" I said, "I'm taking a picture."

He said, "You can't take no pictures around here." So he made me fold my tripod up, but I had already made my exposure by then. I had a time shot of about six seconds and he talked a lot longer than that. I had a bulb in my hand and squeezed it until I was done. Then I let go and he didn't know if I was taking a picture or not.

I did some other work for Mrs. Clarence E. [Hattie] White, who was the first black school board member. And I met a white guy down there, and he'd said he was a writer. He said, "I'd like to get with you to send a story to *Ebony.*" So, after I developed the prints, he came by and picked up some pictures and he mailed them to *Ebony* magazine. I think he wrote the story, and told me to send them the pictures and how much to charge for them. "And when you get the check you can just send me half of it." He was from somewhere in Dallas. So when the check came, I mailed him half of it.

A lot of these things happen like that. I took funerals, church services, picnics, just anything. If somebody wanted me to shoot a picnic, I had to try to get some idea of what news value the pictures were, for one thing. And it took me a long time to figure that out because I used to make a lot of pictures and say, "Well, this isn't news value. Why didn't you take it this way or that way?" Then I began to learn what they were looking for in news pictures and then I tried to capture that. Most of the time I was out there getting paid. I used to ask the people, "What do you want?" And they'd set up their scene, whatever scene they want. That's what I would shoot, nothing else.

You see, some organization would send me up to the Eldorado Ballroom to take pictures. And any time a radio station or a newspaper would send me up to take a picture, they always wanted crowds in the advertising. They wanted lots of people in it. Sometimes the radio station would sponsor something out there, and they'd want a picture of the scene or crowds. I shot pictures for KCOH ever since they were almost first in existence.

Sometimes there's a sense of humor in the photographs, like when I took the photograph of the kids at the Eldorado Ballroom. The kids said, "Take my picture! Take my picture!" I had no idea that this picture would be anything other than a snapshot. I might have told them, "Well, what am I going to do with it?" They'd say, "I want it, I want it," but they wouldn't get it unless they paid me and I mailed it to them.

I used to come up there a lot of times just on a hustle. I could walk into the Eldorado and they'd say, "Mr. Joseph, do you got your camera?" And I'd say, "Yeah, it's down in the car." So people would be partying up there and they'd want pictures made.

Well, I didn't know too much about selling photographs, and I was possessed to be a writer. I never did have time to sit down and do writing, nothing like that. Some people thought I should do write-ups for the paper, but I was never gifted for that.

The Houston *Informer* would call me when they needed me. They never had a photographer on their staff. They did eventually. They hired Hiram Dotson. He was a photographer. He was in a class ahead of me, but they made an engraver out of him.

I don't consider myself an artist. I'm just a picture-taker. The reason why I say that is that I've been to seminars, and they tell you what you see in a person. You can talk with him, but

I'm not much of a talker, but they say if you talk with a person, then you can bring out his character. You can see it in him in his conversation. I could never see all of that in it. I'd sit a person down and I would just use the basic photography on him, give him a little Rembrandt lighting or something like that. I guess I just don't understand art. I look at a photograph and read the description of what it is.

I just wasn't creative in that way. I was interested in action. I never did like a picture that was posed, or somebody looking at me. I wanted to catch that action and the way I did it came natural. The only thing I'd be thinking about is how to compose it. Sometimes I'd be in a hurry and more of the composing would take place in the printing, how I cropped and framed it. Sometimes I'd take side shots that show more action in the audience and environment, but people wouldn't buy them. They wanted tight profiles.

I couldn't always get the depth of field I wanted, so I would get as much as I could. I'd pick the point of focus that showed what I was after.

I worked for this guy, Provost. I thought he could come up with ideas that I thought were kind of artistic. It's something I would not have thought of if I was taking the pictures. I don't remember any incidents, but I do remember having the thoughts that way.

My primary interest was in making a buck, and I got kind of discouraged because I didn't think black people really cared anything about the art of photography. I can recall when I used to want to use a Rembrandt lighting on people, they complained that one side was too dark. So the creativity I had about lighting just began to disappear. You just gave them flat lighting and they seemed to be more satisfied and that's what sold them. I think they were not educated about photography. They didn't want to know why one side was dark and the other was not. They just wanted it to look the same.

I've done a little commercial work for white photographers, and the thing they seem to be interested in is getting something done real cheap. I've done things for advertising agencies when they got a client that didn't want to spend a lot of money. Then they look you up. So when I ask for more business, they never come around again. The people there doing business get on their feet and you don't hear from them any more.

I'm semi-retired now. The only thing I do now is work for organizations, sororities; a few business places use me. There are social and political affairs. I used to do debutante balls, a lot of banquets. I did a lot of political work. I did a lot of work for Barbara Jordan when she was starting out. I did portraits for her. When they got her to run for the Texas Senate, they had these big affairs at these hotels. And I've done work for the local people, Councilman Hall and Mickey Leland.

I did a lot of pictures of formals and affairs for fraternities and sororities. I belong to a fraternity, Phi Beta Sigma. I joined it in 1959. I had been taking pictures for them for a long time and they invited me to join. It was mainly a social organization, but we did community service.

I can remember when I first started taking pictures. I could take a group picture and sell everybody a picture because nobody had photographs of themselves. Nobody had cameras. Usually I'd position the flash right over the camera where the shadow would fall down or behind the person. But with the background dark, the shadow wouldn't show up. I'd hand-hold the flash at a high angle to eliminate the shadow. I taught myself to do flash photography. Teal used lights, except when he used a panoramic camera. I used a bulb flash and then in 1968 I got a strobe flash.

I've used view cameras, 8x10 portrait cameras with 5x7 and 4x5 backs on them. We used to shoot 5x7 and 4x5 film on portraits. I've used a 2¼, a Pentax. I've had a lot of stuff stolen from me. I used to use a roll film camera with a 70mm lens. I'd shoot anything with that, portraits, school work.

I had one studio on Wheeler and then one on Blodgett. From July of 1958 to July of 1968 I was at 3505A Wheeler. I lived in the Sunnyside area at that time. I worked for Herbert Provost for awhile prior to getting that studio. That was from 1950 to 1953. We didn't have a contract, just a gentleman's agreement. I worked with him between 1950 and 1953, until right after I got married.

I've been married since 1953. My wife's name is Hattie. She was from the Fifth Ward area. Her maiden name was Calbert. I have a daughter, Detra; two sons in the middle and a

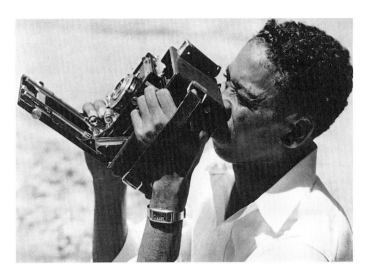

Unknown maker, *Benny Joseph*, Houston, Texas, ca. 1950s.

daughter on each end. Her name is Damita. One of my sons is named Benny A. Jr. and the other is Roderick.

I bought my house on Rio Vista in 1968, the year TSU bought the building that I was in on Wheeler. The building belonged to the Groovy Grill and they bought them out. Then I paid rent to TSU until they decided to tear the building down.

So I had to vacate and the move was expensive. It was kind of rough. This had been a Jewish area. Since they wouldn't let the Jews move into River Oaks, they built up their own River Oaks in this area around MacGregor. Then the Jews moved out to the suburbs in an area off West Loop. A lot of these Jewish temples were bought by the Baptists. That happened all over the city.

When the blacks started moving out here, it wasn't peaceful at all. They bombed the houses they lived in. I used to live on Alabama Street. That was the border line. Between Alabama and Riverside there was a block of nothing but brush and weeds. They didn't build anything on that block. Some of the families sold their homes.

I had the studio at 2305 Blodgett from 1968 to 1982. I did portrait sittings, display sittings, anything I had to shoot. I had a workroom for drying, stamping, and drying pictures, a darkroom, and a retouching room. In the studio I painted the walls a bluish color. When I was on Wheeler Street I had to use a backdrop because

I had a heater in the back of the sitting room. Then I used a gray backdrop. I had rolls of paper that I could unroll when I needed it. When I took portraits, I used such a wide lens that the background was out of focus. With the musicians I had to use a short-focus lens and got a large depth of field. That's why I picked up the background that I did.

The large lens I used was a 127mm. I had a roll film camera, a Camarez that had a 70mm or 90mm lens. I never used the 90mm, only 70mm. It had a 4x5 back. With the musicians I used 4x5. Sometimes I used 2 ¼. I had a photogenic light setup, a power pack with four outlets. Sometimes I used a diffusing screen. I'd have fill-in, a main source, a highlight, and a backlight.

I never did shoot much on speculation. I charged twenty-five dollars for an assignment and five-fifty for a print, but it was understood that I owned my negatives. I was furnishing the film and all supplies.

When I shot a portrait, I used matte paper. Since color was out, you had to use what they make. Today, all I use is color film. If I want black-and-white, I make it. If they want color, I can have it done.

The only prints I made were the ones people requested, other than of course what I did for my family and friends. Some of these I never thought would be printed. I always used a cream-colored fiber paper. The black tones are deeper and more subtle. I used selenium toning for permanence, but also sometimes to alter the coloring of the print in portraits.

I made my money doing school pictures, that was 85 to 90 percent of all my work. Then in 1968 I got out of the school business. Things had changed. Kickbacks were asked for. Then integration killed it. I used to shoot all of these little country schools, go out South Main, Beaumont highway, and then they integrated all the black high schools with white students. They made junior highs out of the black high schools and the white principals wouldn't hire me. That was real disappointing at the time because I was making money. Then I decided I could make my living some other way. I had plans made up for an elaborate studio that had three printing rooms, retouching rooms, but it never came to be.

I didn't find photography to be a get-rich gimmick, but I've made a decent living out of it.

Benny Joseph, *NAACP Regional Meeting*, Houston, Texas, ca. 1960s.

Benny Joseph, *Barbara Jordan*, Houston, Texas, 1964.

Benny Joseph, *KCOH Downtown Parade*, Houston, Texas, ca. 1960s.

Benny Joseph, *Yates Prom, May 18, 1956,* Houston, Texas.

Benny Joseph, *Lost Boy*, Houston, Texas, ca. 1960s.

202

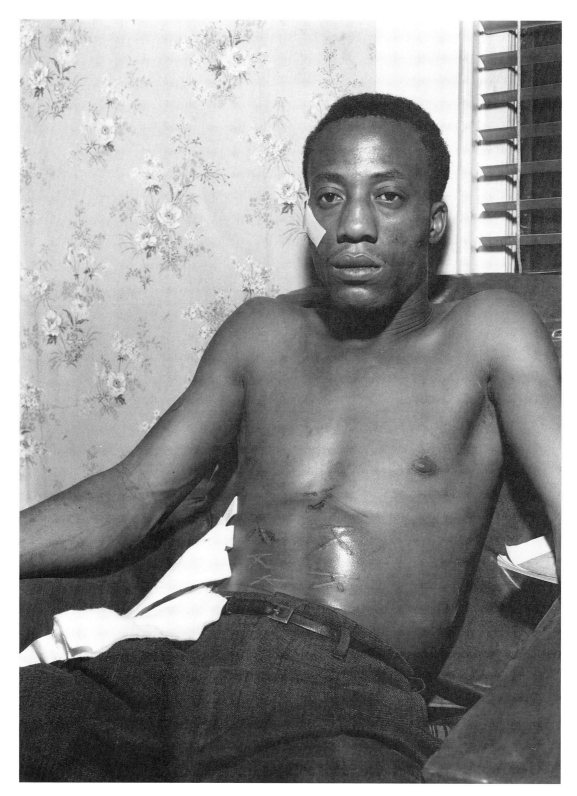

Benny Joseph, *Felton Turner*, Houston, Texas, 1960.

Benny Joseph, *KCOH Promotion*, Houston, Texas, ca. 1960s.

Benny Joseph, *KCOH Promotion*, Houston, Texas, ca. 1960s.

Benny Joseph, *Martin Luther King Jr.*, St. John Baptist Church, Houston, Texas, ca. 1960s.

Benny Joseph, *Thurgood Marshall*, Antioch Baptist Church, Houston, Texas, ca. 1960s.

Benny Joseph, *NAACP Parade*, Houston, Texas, 1976.

Francis Williams*

I've been active in the NAACP since 1951 when I started practicing law. I'm originally from Austin. I'm sixty-four years old now. I went to law school at Howard University in Washington, D.C. When I applied to go to law school in 1946, there was no place to go to in Texas, being black. So I started writing around the country to law schools. I got admitted to Howard and to a couple of others, but I chose Howard. I graduated with the class of 1950.

I was a reservist and I got recalled to active duty during the Korean conflict. I went back on active duty in September 1950 and stayed until October 1951. I bought a car and came to Houston to start practicing law with Henry Doyle.

I had a general practice years ago, but I have restricted that now. I spent a short period on the bench in the criminal court. So now that I'm back in private practice, I restrict my activity to criminal law, probate, and family law. You cannot keep up with all of the law. Every time I try to keep up with law I get myself in trouble.

I was involved in several of the civil rights cases that were filed here in Houston. The two major ones that I participated in were the courthouse cafeteria suit of 1953, and then in 1956, the day after Christmas, Mr. Doyle (who later became a judge) and I filed the Houston Independent School District desegregation suit, *Ross* v. *Rogers.*

In 1956 there were several parents who took their children to the closest school. Those close schools happened to be white schools and of course their children were denied admission because the schools were designated white or colored. The parents called the NAACP and told me what happened: "I took my child to such and such a school and talked to the principal and she said that she had instructions from the school board office that no colored were to be enrolled." So I was quoted in the media as saying that the school board should follow the law of the land and admit children to the local schools. And one Saturday I looked out the front door. I lived in the Sunnyside area at the time. I was doing something in the house, and a cross was burning in the front yard. Where I lived was not in the city of Houston proper. It was in Harris County, so the sheriff had jurisdiction.

Several people asked me if I was scared. Hell, no, I was mad. I ran and got my rifle, but they were long gone. As a matter of fact, when I went out the front door and looked, there was nobody up and down the street. They were gone. Of course, the neighbors and the volunteer fire department, we put the thing out with a water hose. And the sheriff was called and they came out and took it. I immediately began to get calls from newspapers and television stations. I remember one person called and said, "You Francis Williams? What's going on out there?"

"Nothing unusual."

"Okay."

They had called up all these stations and the night editor of the *Post* called and said, "They tell me some fool done set a burning cross in your front yard."

And I said, "They did."

He said, "Well, what are you going to do about it?"

"What do you mean, 'do about it'?" I said, "Hell, they're gone."

And he asked, "What's your reaction?"

"It's racial bigots."

---

* Interview with Francis Williams (April 23, 1922–August 22, 1993) by Alan Govenar, September 5, 1987.

He said, "Did they come close to the house?"

I said, "I don't know, because I didn't see them."

And he said, "What would you have done if you had seen them?"

I said, "I would have probably shot them." I said, "Look, I don't want you to run that in the paper." I was President of the local NAACP from 1954 to 1959.

So the other newspapers called. The *Chronicle* even had a picture of it in the paper. So I went down to the sheriff's office to look at it and they had it in the closet with a lot of other things. It was made by a carpenter. The cross-piece was not just nailed on, it was mitered. And there was a railroad spike in it to stick it in the ground. It had been carefully planned. Of course, it upset my wife very much.

I built a practice by going to civic club meetings and handing out cards. Almost every night I'd go to somebody's civic club and they would always let me say something because there weren't many black lawyers. I'd make a little speech. Well, being gone, my wife was upset. She wouldn't leave. She wouldn't go stay with anybody. So a friend of mine, an electrician, came out and put lights on the corners of the house. The lights would light up both sides. I never had any problem. They never came back.

When I was preparing the courthouse cafeteria suit, my telephone used to ring. I'm listed, always have been. As long as I'm a lawyer, I'll be listed. Well, they called me up and cursed me out and called me "Nigger, nigger, nigger," and I'd just hang up. And sometimes I'd get tired of that, and I'd cuss them out. My wife was horrified, but I'd cuss them out. I'll never forget one guy who called one Saturday. He was working at some kind of place that I could hear machinery in the background and he called. We were just talking about integration and he was saying how black folks shouldn't go to school with white folks. And I was trying to tell them that they're all children, and they all needed to learn. Then he'd hang up. Every hour on the half hour he'd call. So I told my wife, "Let's look at the late show," and so we sat up until about one o'clock and he called, but at two-thirty I was in bed asleep. I said, "Now don't call me any more. I'm tired of talking to you. I've been talking to you all night. To hell with you and you go on about your business."

He said, "We been talking all night, but you haven't cussed me."

I said, "I don't want to cuss you."

So we had a cussing spree. You see, I was a child who went to school during the Depression. In Austin we used to have a lot of caustic rhymes we used to say with each other, very foul language. I started reciting some of those to him. And all he could say was "Why, you nigger! Why, you nigger!"

And I'd say something that insulted his female relatives. They used to call it "playing the dozens." And he never heard that, I'm sure. As soon as I'd say one, I'd think of another. I haven't thought of most of those in years, but he didn't call back.

Usually when they'd call, we'd have a discussion, although heated, about integration. They didn't call it desegregation. They called it integration. I used to get a lot of bad telephone calls when I was president of the NAACP.

In the first case, the courthouse cafeteria suit took about a year. The second case was filed the day after Christmas in 1956, and we tried it in 1957. But the case lasted almost thirty years on the docket. Mr. Doyle and I tried it, but after a period of time we were no longer associated with it. You see, the NAACP was put out of business in 1957 in Texas.

The State of Texas alleged that the NAACP was a foreign corporation and not governing its business properly in registering as a foreign corporation and making reports to the state. There was a major lawsuit about that in Tyler, Texas. Why did they choose Tyler? I don't know why they chose Tyler, but I think it was because it was a hotbed of racial biases in East Texas.

A compromise in the Tyler case came after about a year and a half. The NAACP was back in business.

People had not been meeting publicly. A judge had issued a temporary restraining order that forbade the NAACP to meet. So there were other organizations that tried to assume the mantle, but most of them didn't get off the ground. They were not as viable as the NAACP.

The courthouse cafeteria case was one that got a lot of us to thinking in Texas. As the junior person in the office it was my chore to do the research on the courthouse cafeteria suit. I found two cases in 1953 dealing with public accommodation. One was a swimming pool case in Lima, Ohio, and the other was an NAACP-sponsored suit for Virginia Beach, Virginia. It seems that in the Virginia Beach case, there was a certain part of the beach set aside for coloreds. (That's what we were called then. That was way before we were "black.") And the NAACP brought a lawsuit because of the city ordinance that they should be allowed to use the entire beach. That case I found in the federal courts. The other case I found was the Ohio state courts. It was concerned with a swimming pool near a black area. If you have ever been in the North, there was residential segregation. Well, the city fathers decided to build an Olympic-sized swimming pool in a more affluent area. So black folks went out there to swim, but they wouldn't let them swim. But you see, Ohio had an anti-segregation law since the Civil War days, and that case was decided on state law, rather than on constitutional grounds as the Virginia Beach suit.

Doyle and I talked about the research that I had done and we found out that everything in that courthouse cafeteria was bought by Harris County—the dishes, the plates, the pots and the pans, the seats. There was a concessionaire, a person who leased it, but everything there was paid for by the county. We sued the county judge in a commissioner's court. We tried that case for three days over in the federal court. That case was decided in our favor, but it was appealed by the county, of course, in the Fifth Circuit. I did not, however, at that time have my certificate to practice law before the Fifth Circuit Court in New Orleans. I did send in my money so that I could go to New Orleans to argue it. They heard it in Fort Worth, and that was a great comedown. Two judges from the circuit came and they affiliated one of the district judges and they heard the case. They decided to affirm the lower court action. Again the county appealed to the Supreme Court of the United States. The Supreme Court of the United States denied it. So we a had a mini-rout down there when we went to eat the next day. They let the decision stand.

The *Ross* v. *Rogers* suit was finally dismissed about a year and a half ago, in 1986. All cases were under the continuous supervision of the courts to see that they complied. The basis of that case was that they denied entrance to black children to go to so-called white schools.

White schools happened to be closer to them than the black schools. They had to travel a longer distance to the black schools.

Years later, there was a story in the local papers about the events of that time and how the case was finally dismissed. One of the papers found one of the plaintiffs and she was grown and had children who were ten or eleven years old. She was a fifth-grader when she was a plaintiff with her parents, however.

Today you can go to the school closest to your home. Legally, the case was resolved because they eventually changed the rules. There were a lot of obstacles, and there still are some. People were pretty cohesive back then. We had a cadre of people who joined the NAACP and contributed money.

Let me tell you a story that I told the attorney general that came down to speak to the black lawyers' group about ten years ago. We had a dinner meeting and asked the attorney general to speak to the Houston Lawyers Association. We couldn't join the Houston Bar Association in those days, so we formed our own organization. In any case, the attorney general was there and I was asked to make some remarks. I told him that we had trouble with one attorney general back during the 1950s. He was the one who initiated the NAACP lawsuit. They sent agents from the attorney general's office all over the state to seize the records of the NAACP in the various cities. That injunction was issued one day in Tyler, and the next morning when we first learned anything about it, some people went to the NAACP office to start looking through the records. Mrs. Adair was executive secretary of the NAACP at that time and she called me. Of course, I didn't know anything about it and she said, "It's on the radio. Turn on the radio." And there was a flash every half-hour that this action had been taken. They had done it all over the state. Everybody wanted to call Durham in Dallas. W. J. Durham was the leader of the NAACP lawyers in Texas. He was a lawyer with whom Thurgood Marshall associated in the Texas cases. And on this day no one could get through to Durham. The lines were so busy. Every one was trying to call him. They wanted membership lists and contributor lists. Those are the main things they wanted, but they had to reckon with Mrs. C. D. Adair. Mrs. Adair was very feisty, but she was a horrible bookkeeper. Things were not that orderly. Her office looked worse than my desk. So they said, "Where are the membership lists?"

She said, "We don't have any membership lists." And of course they didn't believe her. But she didn't type but hunt and peck, and she didn't keep a running roster. What she did was to keep the duplicates of the lists she sent to New York. If you put them together, you could finally figure out who was a member, but she didn't keep a running roster.

I found out later that they [the agents] were from the comptroller's office. And we decided that under no circumstances could we allow the Houston list to get in the hands of the attorney general. Not that we had too many white people in the NAACP, but we had some and we had a lot of teachers, a lot of people who worked in jobs. And we figured that if that list became public, these people were going to lose their jobs. That happened in some places. So after they had been there two whole days, we talked to Mrs. Adair. Every once in a while they asked her questions and she gave them a short answer. She was very uncooperative with them. I spent a half a day over there, the first day, talking with them, awaiting word from on high from New York [where the national NAACP office was located], but the only word we got was that they had a temporary restraining order to proceed.

So I looked at the attorney general and I told him that I got a key from Mrs. Adair and we went over there in the middle of the night. She told us exactly where those membership records were, exactly where the contribution records were, and we took them out in the middle of the night. And on the next day I burned them. I said, "I can tell you that, sir, because the statute of limitations has run against me." The lawyers there at the meeting went crazy. The statute of limitations had run against my action back in 1957. It was 1979, '80 or something, and they whooped it up.

Somebody told me that they had a photograph of me walking a picket line at Texas Southern graduation in May 1956. Photographs in those days could be used as evidence in court, for both sides. You see, I was president of the local NAACP branch and we decided we should picket the commencement because

Governor Alan Shivers was the speaker. Alan Shivers had expressed his opposition to the 1954 decision of *Brown* v. *Board of Education.* So we labeled him a segregationist and picketed him.

We talked about it at the NAACP board meeting. We met every Thursday night, usually at a church somewhere, Third Ward this week, Akers Home next week, Sunnyside, all over the city. We had a cadre of about fifteen people who would come to the meeting irrespective to where it was. But we'd pick up people from those neighborhoods. We'd usually have fifty to sixty people, but when the issues were hot we had more than that.

We decided at the board meeting to picket and we took it to the membership and they agreed with us. We sent somebody for some poster boards. I wanted to look at all the signs. I wanted to be sure that they were not in poor taste. So they made signs that Saturday, and the word got out. Somebody said there was a law against picketing, and I had to hit the law books. I didn't know of any law, but I had to check, and all I found was something concerning the number of pickets at a union strike.

One woman was concerned about how it might affect her son. But we picketed and we had a parade of people along Wheeler Avenue to come to see the signs. We were on TV.

The signs said everything from "Down with Shivers" to "Segregation Must Go," and things that were related to his stand on public schools and desegregation.

There were lots of people taking pictures from the black media. The news services, AP or UPI, took pictures. But not much really changed because the [desegregation] suit was still in limbo. The school board tried a lot of end-arounds. For example, they established the brother and sister rule, that one child could not go to an integrated school if another child was going to an all-black school. In other words, brothers and sisters had to attend the same school. That had to be appealed. Henry Doyle and I were out of the case then. The NAACP had stepped in. They tried several devices. Finally, the school board changed and there was a lessening of impediments that were put in the way of students.

Hattie Mae White was the first black school board member and that was in 1954. She and I were on television when the school board debated the integration issue. That was before she was a school board member. The school board was an entertainment once a month on television. They had a greater viewership for that than any other program, but they wanted to delete it because it got to be too much.

Weldon Berry was the black attorney who completed the school board suit. M. W. Plummer was the plaintiff in the courthouse cafeteria suit. We wanted him to be a lawyer, but he wanted to be a plaintiff. We honored him by putting his name first, rather than in alphabetical order. So that the case is on the books as *M. W. Plummer and others* v. *Bob Casey*, who was a county judge.

Weldon Berry also represented plaintiffs in other small districts. Joe Reynolds split from that firm that had the school suit and he made a specialty of defending school boards in desegregation suits all over East Texas. Joe Reynolds was very conservative. He said, "I don't how many of you have money enough to send your children to private school, but I don't have any money. I'm going to have to send my children to a public school because I can't afford to send my daughters to a private school." He was saying that his children would not go to school with black people. Well, his daughters didn't probably have to do that because the case was in court so long that they had probably finished. Nothing was done about housing segregation until the 1970s. And housing discrimination was rampant. I understand a lot of young couples would go beyond the housing projects in southwest Houston, and they would be told, "We don't have any apartments for rent."

The Sweatt case was one of the most important precedents for what followed. It was tried in Austin in 1946. At that time, the law was that suits like that had to be filed in state court. You had to exhaust your state remedy and then go from district court to the appellate court to the state supreme court and then, and then only, could you file it in the federal system.

The local NAACP Houston branch initiated the suit because Sweatt was a postal carrier in the city. W. J. Durham was the attorney. He represented Heman Marion Sweatt. He just passed away. He became a social worker in Atlanta.

The case concerned his admission to the University of Texas Law School. I read about it in the Austin *American-Statesman*. I was thinking about going to law school. So I strolled on up to the courthouse. I got there about ten. I saw a couple of people standing outside. I saw a big burly man. I just knew he was a police officer. There was a demeanor about him. I went to reach for the door, and he said, "You can't go in there!"

I looked and said, "Why?"

And he flushed and he said, "Because it's full." And I saw the other people looking at me. I don't know why. I wasn't trying to be testy with him. So I just stood there and at twelve o'clock the old double doors opened and everybody came out—Thurgood Marshall and W. J. Durham and some other big-shot Austin, Texas, folks. They all came out and went to lunch, and somebody told me it was going to be recessed to one o'clock. So I went in and took a seat and when they opened back up I had a seat. It was very boring. They were reading statistics into the record, no flesh and blood testimony or anything. For example, they stated how many black people were in Texas, how many were going to Prairie View.

I went to Sam Huston, what's now called Huston-Tillotson. Sam Huston was a small Methodist school, and there was another small all-black school in Austin supported by the Congregationalist church, called Tillotson. The smartest thing they ever did was merge back in the late 1940s. I was an undergraduate from 1940 to 1944. Then I went to the war. I got deferred for about a year. I graduated and I was going to be a doctor. I had applied to Howard and Meharry, the only black medical schools in the country, and didn't get in. My draft board consisted of one man. He told me, "We're going to give you boys at Sam Huston and Tillotson the same break we give to boys at the university in Austin."

I said, "Yes, sir, yes, sir."

And he said, "You're going to go to medical school. If not, you got to go to Raleigh." I didn't get in and thirty-six days later, I got my greetings and went into the service.

After I got out, I applied to law school and was admitted to Howard. The *Sweatt* case started that summer, and I was in law school at Howard when the *Sweatt* case was argued in the Supreme Court of the United States. It was argued in 1948 and the whole law school went there, but it wasn't finally decided in his favor until 1950.

Sweatt went to law school. Of course, they punched him out quickly. He failed. Well, I understand that some professors would call on him everyday. It's difficult to brief cases for five professors everyday. He was an excellent plaintiff by virtue of his personal history, no arrests. He was a graduate of Wiley College. He was a postman, paid his taxes. He was married. There was nothing on him. They wanted somebody who was squeaky clean in a case like that. He was mature, but he had been out of college for fourteen years and that made it very difficult.

Some of Papa's friends urged me to wait for the *Sweatt* case to be resolved. One said, "You could live at home. It would be much cheaper," but money didn't bother me. I had the G.I. Bill. So, after I got admitted, I got on the train and went to Washington.

My papa, Pinckney A. Williams, was an agent for a black-owned insurance company called American Woodman. He was also a real estate agent and a notary public. We lived in a mixed neighborhood, poor whites, poor blacks, and poor Mexicans all in the same block in Austin. But Papa was the only businessman on the block. Papa wore a white shirt with a detachable starched white collar everyday. Papa always had a car. A lot of the people in our neighborhood didn't have cars. When they brought gas in, for example, in the late 1930s, we were one of the three people on the block who had gas.

Papa was what they called a "race man" because he had been active in a lot of civic affairs during his lifetime. We were taught never to trust white folks. We had no white people who came to our house to collect any money or anything. Papa got his own ice. He went to the creamery and bought his own milk. We had no deliveries from anybody. And so I grew up not trusting anybody. I never had a white doctor or dentist put his hands on me until I went to the Army during World War II.

Before I was born Papa had been involved in what the NAACP called the Shillady incident. John Shillady was the secretary of the NAACP and he was white. He came to Austin to fight against the city's order that a local NAACP chapter disband. Well, he was met at the train station by the law enforcement people. He was

marched to the Driskill Hotel and they beat him unmercifully, and then they marched him back to the next train. He didn't have a ticket on the train and he died later from his injuries. There was quite a turmoil in the black community because the word was out that they were going to lynch these people who were going to meet with him. So Papa, I'm told, found out about it and hid out for four days down on the river. They say he took a flour sack and canned goods, a can opener, his shotgun, his pistol, and he left home. Now I was not born. This happened back in the early 1900s. I wasn't born until 1924, but my sisters all knew about it. Well, I didn't hear anything more about that until I became president of the local NAACP and was at a national meeting and somebody mentioned the Shillady incident. In the history of the NAACP there is a reference to what happened in Austin, Texas.

Three years ago, I got a call on the bench. I didn't take calls, I told the clerk, unless it's my wife (and I knew she would not call except for an emergency) or unless it was from another judge or another elected official in the county. I think it is the height of impropriety for a judge to be talking on the telephone while a case is going on, but I've seen them do it. After I got off the bench, they gave me the call and it was somebody from Austin. That evening I called her, and I didn't get an answer. Then my sister called and told me I was going to get a call from a white woman who wanted to know something about Papa. She didn't give her the time of day. She grew up with that attitude that we don't talk to white folks. We didn't tell them anything. Well, when I found out this lady was from the historical society, I got in touch with her on the next day. They were putting together a history of East Sixth Street and they kept on running across the name P. A. Williams. She wanted to know if I had any papers or pictures of Papa. I told her what I had and she was interested. I called up my sister and said, "This is not a hatchet job they want to do about Papa. This is historical."

She said, "Well, you can handle it." In Austin they took what was the colored library and made it into a museum. They put together an exhibit on black businesses in Austin and featured Papa in a prominent manner. Papa was born in Brazoria and his father, I understand, was a Reconstruction-days deputy sheriff and he was poisoned with some milk. Grandma, I understand, took her three children and left immediately and went to San Antonio. They stayed there for a while, but then they came to Austin. My mother was a farm girl from down Lockhart. Papa's first wife had passed away and he met my mother at some meeting or association where she was teaching school. Her name was Buna Williams and she died in 1964. Papa passed away in 1943 and at that time I think he was sixty-three years old. The NAACP was not an active organization in Austin when I was growing up. I think the Shillady incident and other things like that had affected people in an adverse way.

Thurgood Marshall came to Houston about once a year. Thurgood was a lively storyteller and he was much in demand as a speaker. Of course, he was busy raising funds for the NAACP.

We didn't have any political leaders, except persons with the NAACP. We didn't have any public officials outside of the people in New York and Chicago. We didn't have any public officials in California. There were no black elected public officials in Texas, and still there's not too many.

Barbara Jordan was very important during this period. She ran against Willis Watley in 1952 countywide for state representative and lost badly. She ran against the same man in 1954 and lost. Watley was a conservative, but in 1955, as a result of the 1950 census, there had to be redistricting mandated by the law. I sat on the committee. I was appointed by one of the commissioners. There were five blacks on the redistricting committee. At that time the eighteenth senatorial district was conceived and we had a lot of union help. There were few so-called liberal democrats and we carved out the eighteenth district for a black person, right down the middle of the county. We took in a lot of the Fifth Ward, some of the North Side, this area [Third Ward], Sunnyside, and we took in a majority of the black folks. We took in a great enough area so that a black person could win. Of course, Barbara ran for that seat. She was unopposed. No Republican would dare run. And Barbara Jordan won in 1956. She was from the Fifth Ward area.

Barbara graduated from the Boston University Law School, and from Texas Southern in liberal arts. She was on the debating team. After she left for Congress, Greg Washington ran for her seat in the state senate.

The year Barbara was elected state senator, a black, Curtis Graves, was elected state representative. That same year, a black was elected in Dallas. Three people were elected that year because of redistricting. Francis Williams has a theory. You see, we were bound together geographically and we supported each other because we couldn't move to southwest Houston. We couldn't go out and rent an apartment in southwest Houston. The young people rented apartments over here. Crime was not as rampant as it is now.

You knew the people around. Mrs. Adair was known and respected. They knew she was the NAACP lady. People might not know her name, but they knew who she was. We had a strong sense of community pride about us in those days. Nowadays, the youngsters can't wait until they graduate from high school and get any kind of job, girls and boys. Well, the boys want to get a car first, but the girls want to get themselves an apartment. They want to get away from home. They won't live over here in Third Ward. They won't live in Fifth Ward. They want to move out to southwest Houston. Well, the better apartments are in southwest Houston, because there have been no nice apartments built over here, that's for sure. The developers say they don't pay. So that pride that you talk about was fostered because of segregation. We were lumped together. Black businesses thrived.

There were also Jews who lived in this area of Houston. There's a school on Palm that was a synagogue. The True Light Baptist church was also a synagogue.

I tell you how that came about. In their haste to keep the black folks out of the University of Texas, they were seeking some land on which to build a colored law school. And they found some vacant land over here on Wheeler Street. That land was a kind of buffer between the whites on this side of Blodgett Street. All of that was vacant land, and, you see, the blacks stopped at Alabama. Blacks didn't live on Truxillo. So they stuck Texas Southern over there. I have mixed feelings about that, but I don't want to go into it. This caused the Jewish neighbors here some unrest, and they were just not used to having black people walk through the community, unless it was on the way to work, a woman getting off the bus with a white uniform on. So I think the presence of TSU started white flight.

There was one act of violence. A fellow who had quite a bit of money, a cattleman, had a cross burned in front of his house on Wichita, over toward Dowling. You see, blacks were coming this way and there were for-sale signs up all over the neighborhood. That's when Mr. Meyer went out and bought about a hundred acres of land in southwest Houston (it wasn't Houston then) and established Meyerland. He couldn't build those houses fast enough for the people to get out of here.

Houston, however, was unlike a lot of cities in the South in that blacks were able to get loans to buy these houses. They couldn't do it in Atlanta unless they borrowed the money from the black bank in the city. In Houston blacks could get loans from white insurance companies, mortgage companies. They were able to get financing, like I did for this house. Houston was just one of the entrepreneur-type cities. They wanted money. Everybody got a premium price for these houses. I looked at many houses before I found one. This one apparently had been foreclosed on by the mortgage company. I bought this house from the insurance company that owned it in Austin.

There was not much violence, and we should be proud of that. My view is that we didn't have violence that they had in some of the other cities because black folks here could get a job. It might not pay but a dollar an hour, but they had a job. We didn't have a great unemployment problem like they did in some cities.

There were some very successful black businessmen. Don Robey was one of them. I didn't know him well. I went to his night club and I knew that he had his recording business and ties to a lot of gospel groups and blues. He was very successful.

The music was very popular because a lot of people listened to the radio. Radio was and is very important. I'm dismayed that no black person has been able to get into this immediate area with an FM station because all of these youngsters are listening to FM.

I used to do a little [legal] work for Lightnin' Hopkins, but when I met him his friends said he'd slowed down. That was in the early 1970s.

Lightnin's friend and doctor, Dr. Cecil Harold, is an authority on him. He was Lightnin's representative, looked over his contracts and things. He was Lightnin's confidant. I remember when he bought his first Cadillac. He bought a Seville, and Harold talked to me about it. Harold was and still is a great collector and connoisseur of blues records. I used to, but I haven't bought anything in years. I've gotten away from it.

I remember one time Harold and I went to this place right off one of the freeway streets. There was an old theater and Muddy [Waters] was coming. And Lightnin' opened for him. I remember that 90 percent of the persons there were white, mostly youngsters. Right in the middle of things, Harold's beeper went off. He had a woman in labor at St. Joseph's Hospital and he had to leave, but I stayed.

Nobody had much money then. They were working hard. The wages were low, and the music talked to the people. You sang about the blues. I was a great blues man. Not too many white people liked blues then.

Once the blues musicians started going overseas, they were acclaimed in Germany, France, England, and so forth. And the major companies began to take notice of them. All of the older records, on Robey's labels, and others became popular. They called it rhythm and blues.

I went all the way from Miles [Davis] to Muddy. I skipped pop all together. A lot of the social clubs featured the music at their dances. They'd usually have two a year, one that was public and one that was invitational. I was appointed to the county criminal bench in 1985 and I spent about fourteen or fifteen months on the bench. And I left the bench in January 1987. I'm now sixty-four and I'm still practicing law. I've been practicing since October 1951. My steps are slow now. Somebody said, "Why don't you retire?" I don't know what in the world I'd do. I don't play golf. You see, I came along too late for golf. That sounds good, but I got a set of clubs over there in the corner. They're nice clubs. I went to the Oshman's sale and bought some good clubs, shoes, tees, everything, and I've been out three times.

I got a friend who's retired and goes golfing every weekend or more now. Every time he comes over here and sees my clubs, he laughs.

Louise Martin

My mother told me when I left home to avail myself to anything that's good: "If it will help you, you participate in it, but if it's going to hinder you or if somebody's going to harm you, don't have anything to do with it."

I grew up in Brenham, Washington County, Texas. I was born on January 9, 1911, and we did very well for that day and time. We didn't have to go to the country and pick cotton. We were normal kids, normal black kids. There was a lot of mixing that I recall as a child. We did not call it integration. We were not that gracious and we weren't that educated to use those particular words during that time when I was a child. In Brenham there were the Germans and the Dutch, and they're still there, older ones and children all—even though a lot of them have left.

My family did the normal work that most black people did. They were domestic workers; they cooked for the banker or the doctor, someone like that. My father was a bartender; he did what's commonly called domestic work. My parents were Barbara Harris and Vander Martin Harris, and my parents lived in that area for a spell. I remember my grandfather and grandmother very well—Edward Harris and Fanny Harris.

I don't recall my great-grandparents, not that far back. Yes, I do, I'm sorry. It's just that I guess we didn't have them that long, you know, in those days. Older people got arthritis or what they used to call rheumatism. Sometimes I think they lived much longer than we're living now because of a different way of living.

My mother moved to Houston and I went through high school. The schools were definitely segregated and I went on to college,

not right away, but I did. I went to the Art Institute and to Denver University. I was interested in art and always wanted to be a photographer and an artist. I was very good at it as a small child growing up. My mother had a lot of confidence in me and she wanted me to do what I wanted to do. If it meant cutting out paper dolls that would keep us out of trouble, she'd have us doing that.

I was just intrigued with photographs. Anything she saw that was a pretty picture, she brought it to me or bought it for me. And as a child, they sometimes asked me what would I like to be when I grew up, and I didn't even pronounce the word very well, but I had in mind I wanted to be a photographer. I just loved pictures.

I would see the photographers visiting the schools. They were white, possibly German, because most of the Germans were interested in pictures. And I guess that was the only way they could make money. When they visited our schools they would set up a day for our school pictures, which would cost only about twenty-five cents. And on those particular days when we were going to get our pictures made, we'd dress up.

I only saw one picture of my father. My parents were not picture-conscious at that day and time. A German fellow might go around and offer to make pictures. I have copies of many pictures that go way back—old ministers, prominent people with the high collars or whatever was in style. That sort of thing intrigued me and made me feel that I one day could do the same thing.

A lot of families who were our neighbors had tintypes and some even had large portraits that were hung on the wall. The photographer

Pauline Robinson, *Louise Martin*, Houston, Texas, 1949. *Sepia-toned silver gelatin print.*

might encourage them to get an enlargement of their mother or father for just a little more money.

The first black photographer that I met after coming to school in Houston was a Mr. Harris, who made pictures that were a little more modern than what we had seen as we were growing up. And the first black photographer that I really got to know was A. C. Teal. Teal was the popular photographer in the schools, and he even discussed having made the little tintypes or something like that. I couldn't tell you everywhere he went, but I'm certain he went everywhere, because he used to tell us in meetings how little it afforded for food for them to eat. He had made pictures for as little as fifteen or thirty cents.

I must have been about ten or eleven years old when I got my first camera. That was a Kodak view camera, and as I progressed, I got others. After the end of the war, I began to use all Speed Graphic equipment. Up until then,

you couldn't get one. They wouldn't even sell you one unless you were planning on going into photography. I loved the way the Graflex cameras performed and I used them all through my career. I used other cameras, but as long as they made the Speed Graphic, that was my favorite.

For printing, I liked the Eastman Kodak paper. They made a paper that was like velvet. It was called charcoal black. All those names appealed to people, especially to me, because with that paper I could make black folks look prettier. That was my secret to making good prints.

I had planned to open my own studio when I was in school. And I would do pictures for my church or whatever, but during the war years I didn't officially open my own business. I couldn't get a telephone. It wasn't until 1948 or 1949 that I finally opened my studio. That was over on the north side where I lived. It was on Maury Street, not far from my church, the First

United Baptist Church on Lyons Avenue. I married briefly, but he didn't want me in business and that sort of thing. He worked for the railroad company.

I lived out in Fifth Ward during the time I was married. But all the time he was not wanting me to be a businesswoman. He was the conventional-type husband: a woman should be at home with the children. But I did not have any children. And I still was determined to have my own business. So I did the separating.

About 75 percent of my work was portraiture. I also photographed social doings and sororities, such as Zeta Phi Beta and Gamma Phi Delta. Gamma Phi Delta is a business sorority for professional women. I photographed black women lawyers, the Houston League of Business and Professional Women, national and local chapters. And through the art of retouching I learned to make people look much better, and any time you can make a woman that's not pretty look better or prettier, that's your customer, and she will bring you other customers. Probably three-fourths of my customers were women. I could do any kind of photography: professional, commercial, or what have you. I did some work for the *Forward Times* and the *Informer*, the black papers. Carter Wesley had the *Informer*. He was hell-a-mile, but he was good to people who worked for him. He was an attorney, and he was a big man. He wasn't afraid of anybody.

I photographed all kinds of people: Lena Horne, Barbara Jordan, and even three presidents: John Kennedy, Eisenhower, Richard Nixon. I photographed the Martin Luther King funeral. I was doing some journalism for the *Forward Times* and the *Informer* at that time, and they both sent me. I had met King prior to his death, years before, because a college that I worked for, the Hughes Business College, brought him to Houston. And I met Mrs. King in Atlanta.

I've always been associated with the press, and I had bona fide press cards. I even did national press coverage. I worked for insurance companies, and people who were in positions to help me obtain these particular things, plus I studied some journalism along with my photography. I was told by my professor one time

that any good photographer will associate himself with good newspapers. I was a pretty smart woman, not just to make a good picture, but to involve myself and to make talks to children and the like. I did not graduate in journalism, but I studied a good deal of it and I practiced in darkrooms at all the local newspapers, and I was able to help them a lot, and they were able to help me.

People more or less considered me a society photographer, because I worked a lot with women. But I had the knowledge to fit in any situation, and I didn't have to wait or stand on the sidewalk to photograph the mayor or this or that. I excelled over the regular journalism person because I shot it, processed it, and got it to you on time.

I demanded a certain attitude in my studio. I stomped my foot and they would do what I told them. They came to me for service. If you come to me for a photograph, I'm going to make some good proofs for you to select from. Then you leave the rest to me. You don't tell me, "Now, I want this removed and I want this chin lifted." You trust me as your photographer.

They might say, "I had a picture made once and it had a little spot here." I say, "Leave it to me." I did the retouching and the tinting. It depended on the complexion of the person. Someone might say, "My child's not that black. I don't want this." Well, I wouldn't let them get away with that. If he was black, he was black. I didn't overdo it. I would give the picture the desired amount of light to make it look presentable.

I brought lights with me, portrait lights, anything to make good pictures. I tried to avoid people's living rooms, but I would if they couldn't come to the studio. With weddings or receptions, I had helpers.

I wasn't an extravagant woman. I was a dancer, a tap dancer, and I played the marimba. I didn't do it as a professional, but I did it. Anybody who wanted me as a soloist, I would do it—ladies at the Y, the University of Houston. I always had anything I wanted, like clothes and style, all of this. I had a Studebaker with wide tires. And I tried to be the top professional photographer. I've worked very hard and I'm a good Christian.

Louise Martin Art Studios, *Annual Foreign Mission Society Tea, Antioch Baptist Church, Mrs. Vanita Crawford (far left)*, Houston, Texas, ca. 1957–1963. *Courtesy Houston Metropolitan Research Center.*

Louise Martin Art Studios, *Group Portrait of the Matrons of the Mission Society of Antioch Baptist Church,* Seated, left to right: *Mrs. A. W. Mitchell, Irene Doswell, Florence C. Powell, Ollie M. Riley.* Standing, left to right: *Mrs. Orpha Boone, Dorothy Herold, Julia DeHart, Jewell Mease,* Houston, Texas, ca. 1965. *Courtesy Houston Metropolitan Research Center.*

Louise Martin, *Funeral of Martin Luther King Jr.*, Atlanta, Georgia, 1968.

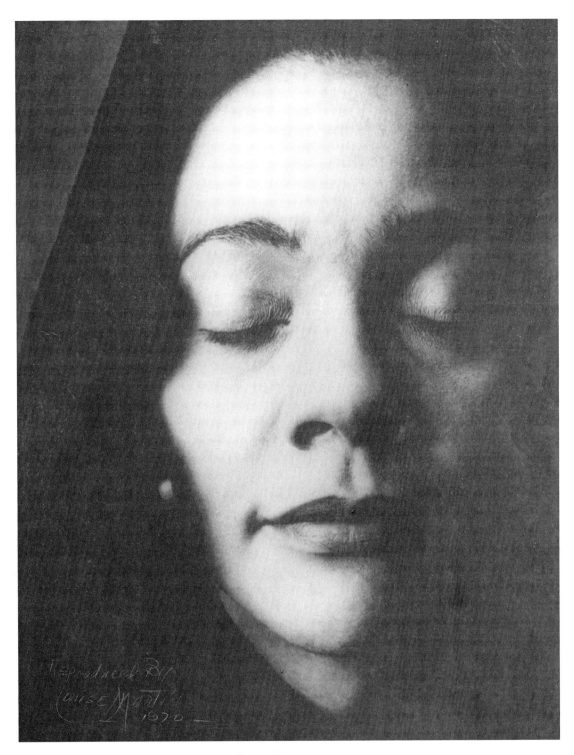

Louise Martin, *Coretta Scott King*, Houston, Texas, 1970.

Rodney Evans

My father was the dean of men at Prairie View College. I was born on January 12, 1922, in Prairie View, and we moved to Houston when I was four years old. And I've spent most of my life here in Houston.

My father taught political science and was the dean of men for years. After we moved to Houston, he worked at an insurance company. I grew up in Houston and started in the Houston public schools. I went to Blackshear and then to Yates, when Yates was where Ryan Junior High is now. And after high school I went to Southern University in Baton Rouge, Louisiana. I went to college in 1941, and into the service in '42 and came back in '46. I graduated in '49, and did some graduate work at Texas Southern and at Sam Houston State in Huntsville. My major was photography, but at that time the photography department at Southern was in the physics department, and during the war it did get exempted for about six months.

I got interested in photography in high school. We had a chemistry teacher, Mr. Farnsworth. I started in chemistry class doing pictures around school, and we set a darkroom up in the hall closet over at Yates. I had a little Kodak camera that my uncle had given my mother, and she let me use it.

Heman Sweatt's nephew was the one who helped me set up my first darkroom at Yates. I remember Heman even before he went to the University of Texas, even before he worked at the post office. The Sweatt family and my family were very close. Heman Sweatt's struggle to get into the University of Texas could have affected me. It would have, especially in law and medicine. The state of Texas would give black students money to go to school out of state because they could not get into any of the law schools in the state of Texas.

I don't think it had that much effect on photography because photography's such an individual thing that it didn't take very much to set it up. So it had very little to do with photography because at that time the blacks had their own lifestyle and what have you. It was just a matter of a person recording that lifestyle.

I can remember a gentleman who I know is the godfather of all black photographers in Texas, and that was Teal. He did photographs at the high schools, and he did all the photographic work down at Prairie View for yearbooks. I remember him from when I was three or four taking a group picture at Prairie View. He was just a great photographer.

I never worked with Teal, but I knew him very well. He took my picture for the first time when I was four years old within a group. Then he made several others at boy scout banquets and things of that nature. The first time I saw flash powder was at a father-and-son banquet years ago at the Pilgrim's Temple. I remember seeing the photograph and it lit up the whole room. Teal was just a super photographer.

I didn't really know very much about Mr. Teal, other than about just his general photography. However, I recall that his brother went into the service, and after he came out, I was in my first year of teaching at TSU. They had a photography program there for veterans and his brother was in that program. He was a tremendous retoucher. In the latter days of Mr. Teal's work and photography, I think his brother did quite a bit of the hand-painting and retouching.

When I started teaching, Teal had a school for photography, but the gentleman who was teaching at TSU at that time was Cliff

Richardson. His father was one of the newspaper publishers here in Houston, and Cliff left TSU to go to Fort Worth to start a magazine. I believe it was called *Sepia* magazine. I was hired at that time to fill in for Cliff. Cliff took a leave of absence, and I was made permanent when he didn't come back.

Cliff's father was the publisher, I think, of the Houston *Informer*. Mr. Richardson was very powerful. He and some of the other people who published the [Houston] *Informer* were really some of the most influential people in Houston.

Sepia was one of the first all-black magazines at that time in Texas and it was a pretty good magazine. I'm sorry that it really didn't hold up longer. Some of the photographers at *Jet* were with Cliff on this magazine. I don't remember any of the photographers, but I do know that two or three photographers were not from Houston, but were from the other areas in Texas. I taught at Texas Southern from January 16, 1952, until 1991. When I started, photography was in the industrial education department. But when I was in school at Southern, photography was under the physics department. At TSU, photography had one of the only air-conditioned buildings on the campus because of the darkroom. I think the only other air-conditioned building was the president's office. I taught about eight courses, from beginners to a course that catered to teachers. We taught news photography and general photography. We had a two-year program that was mostly for veterans who had come out of the service. They might take math and English and photography and get a two-year certificate. Later we moved into a degree program.

The degree program was in industrial education with a major emphasis in photography. And I think students did 124 hours in industrial education and photography. Now the program includes printing and is called graphic arts.

At that time, photography was seen as a craft, not as an art form. We worked quite a bit doing yearbook work and actually doing the photographic work for the university, as well as the teaching. In other words, we more or less photographed the history of the university. I did that just about by myself until probably the late '60s and early '70s and then we started getting student help. We hired Ray Carrington and Earlie Hudnall and some of the other guys that

worked as student assistants. That's how photography really began to grow because those guys were very good photographers and very good students and were very conscientious about what they were doing.

We started out with Speed Graphic cameras. They were really the workhorses; at that time, the so-called Rolls Royce was the Lenhoff. The Lenhoff was a 4x5 press camera, but a lot of people also used it as a portrait camera, as they did with the Speed Graphic.

We used the Omega D enlarger. It was the basic enlarger and it did just about all the work. We were on such a low budget and we got a lot of equipment from the army surplus depot. We had a pretty good connection there, and when they got photographic materials in, they'd give us a call. And we'd go out and look at it and the university was able to purchase it at a reduced price because it was army surplus.

Ninety-nine percent of the chemicals and papers that we used were Kodak. Occasionally, we would use some Agfa, but mainly it was Kodak. We got into RC printing when it first came out, probably in the late '60s and early '70s. Kodak representatives would always come by when there were new materials and give us samples to try out, and we'd let them know how we liked it. RC worked out real well because we were able to do some printing and fixing and washing and drying so fast that we were able to get photographs out so much more quickly. It was really good for us. Before the RC papers came out, we used Kodabromide, and that was a pretty good paper. We had all the grades from zero up to five, but for 90 percent of our negatives we would use Kodabromide two and three.

I didn't teach retouching, but I did teach hand-coloring, which to me was really an art in itself. Ms. Martin and Mr. Provost did some hand-coloring. And there was a man named Cantu, who worked for Teal. To me, he was the master. He was super. I think he did the retouching and hand-painting. He used Marshall oils. That was one of the things our students enjoyed working with.

Once in a while, Ms. Martin would come and do maybe a couple of little lectures, but she never did actually teach at TSU. But she was also a master with the oils, as well as a super photographer.

Most of what we taught was set as a career, not necessarily as art, but really as simply a tool. Most of the youngsters just wanted a career to make money. What it was all about was really not art for art's sake. However, when John Biggers was teaching art at TSU, he required all his art majors to take at least one class in photography. Also, in the early years, most of the pharmacy majors had to take at least one course in photography because at that time when you opened a drug store, you'd always have an area where you sent film out for processing. The pharmacies needed to know if something was bad, what caused it to be bad, so they could talk to their customers as to how to improve.

We didn't go into the history of photography that much. We did a little bit on history in our introductory classes, but our main thing was simply to get a student interested in photography and to get excited about shooting photographs and not just snapshots.

I can remember years ago seeing tintypes and the glass negatives and what have you, but as far as teaching it, no, we did not. The only one that probably did that I would know about would be Mrs. Teal. She may have made tintypes or probably used some glass negatives.

I often wondered how Mr. Teal learned photography, but I don't know. I do know that years ago they did have a school for photography for blacks at the Tuskegee Institute. I don't know whether Mr. Teal had anything to do with that.

Mr. Polk was the photographer at Tuskegee, and Mr. Polk taught the man who taught me at Southern. Mr. Austin retired, I guess, about ten or fifteen years ago. He came there I think from the early '40s. Southern University is in Baton Rouge, Louisiana, and is probably one of the largest black schools in the country—there's Howard, TSU, and Southern, which are three of the largest predominantly black schools in the country.

Most of my work was done at TSU in teaching. At that time the university was growing and 98 percent of my time was spent doing all the photographic work for the university. I just didn't have too much time to do community work, but I did do some. Occasionally, people at the Y might need something. I think Benny Joseph and Provost did quite a bit of work for the YMCA, and I think Ms. Martin also did some work for the YMCA.

I did everything on campus, from check presentations to Martin Luther King and all the celebrities and persons who came to the campus. I remember Jackie Robinson came down for an athletic banquet and Darryl Royal came over to speak at the athletic banquet. Thurgood Marshall came down for the naming of the school, the Thurgood Marshall School of Law. We photographed that. Thurgood Marshall was a very good friend of my mother's best friend. Her maiden name was Ann Robinson, and years ago, when Thurgood came to Houston to work with the NAACP, he stayed with Mrs. Robinson, a black lady who was a very good friend of my family's.

The enrollment in my classes would average about fifty to sixty. Most of the classes had to have ten to fifteen students and we taught three to four classes a semester. It was pretty hectic when you have that many people with only four or five darkrooms to do the work and maybe six or seven cameras, but we did it.

We moved from 4x5 Speed Graphic cameras to 2¼, and then to 35mm in the late '50s, probably about 1959 to '60. We moved to the Rolleiflex and the Canon and the Nikormats and then to Nikons and Hasselblad. There was a 5x7 and an 8x10 camera that were in the department that we taught in portrait class. And at that time we would use the 5x7 and 8x10 to make contact prints.

At the end of the semester students would turn in an album, usually of 5x7 prints, and at the end of the year, we did an exhibition of 8x10 or 11x14 prints. The quality of their albums and the quality of their general work would determine their grade.

In the early '70s we started teaching our first color class. We got enough color to introduce the student and to try to get him interested in color. We taught color processing and printing and the processing of slides and putting slide presentations together. One of my little favorite things that I started years ago was to get students to listen to a record and to do a slide presentation based on the words of the record. It's almost the same thing now that they're doing on television. We'd tell the students that it sounds very easy but it's very difficult to do, especially to do a good job, but we have had some students who did some pretty good work with it.

In 1981 I went to Africa for about week. I went with a group to Lagos, Nigeria. The trip was organized by the president of TSU at the time, Randall Sawyer. It was what we called a trade mission because TSU was trying to set up a work program.

A lot of my students have gone into different areas of photography. Some have gone into commercial photography and medical photography. There's Ray Carrington and Earlie Hudnall who have gone into different things. Earlie is someone who is obviously excellent as a journalist, but is also an art photographer as well.

What kept me going as a teacher was the progress of the students, seeing them grow and mature and actually contribute to the life and history of our area. You never really made big money, but it was just the idea that you were contributing to the public welfare as well as to the education of a young individual.

Rodney Evans, *Photography Students, Texas Southern University,* Houston, Texas, 1961.

Rodney Evans, *Pharmacy Students, Texas Southern University,* Houston, Texas, ca. 1960s.

Rodney Evans, *Basketball Game, Texas Southern University,* Houston, Texas, 1970.

Rodney Evans, *Dr. B. A. Turner, Dr. Samuel N. Nabrit, Dr. Joseph A. Pierce, Texas Southern University,* Houston, Texas, 1962.

Rodney Evans, *Shakespeare Production, Texas Southern University,* Houston, Texas, 1970.

Herbert Provost

I got started in photography when I was in the navy. I was stationed on an aircraft carrier and they had a photography department on board. And I used to talk with one of the guys in that department all the time, and he started taking me in the darkroom. He would develop film and sometimes when he printed aerial maps, I learned from him. He was a very wonderful person, although at the time I was not allowed to be anything in the navy other than a steward or steward mate or a cook. But somehow I was able to see what was going on and pick up all the techniques that I needed to know to develop and print a picture. I was able to get hold of a Kodak Brownie box camera and I started making pictures and developing pictures by myself. I was stationed on an island in the southwest Pacific, and during my spare time I would develop and print pictures. I was able to get paper because my mother would go downtown to the stock house here in Houston and buy paper for me. They would mail it back to me in packages and I printed lots of pictures for different people.

That was in the year of 1944–45, and I was discharged in 1946. When I was discharged, I enrolled in a school in New Haven, Connecticut. It was an artists' school called the Progressive School of Professional Photographers. And I took an eighteen-month course there. Then I returned back to Houston and started working for Mr. Gittings at the Gittings studio. I'd done a year of apprentice work for Mr. Gittings. Then I went to work for Lawless, another commercial photographer. And I worked for Lawless about a year and got a fairly good background in commercial photography. Then I opened up my own business and started my studio at the corner of Dowling and Green in 1949.

I was born in Dayton, Texas, on December 27, 1921. My father and his brothers all moved to Dayton, Texas, from Breaux Bridge, Louisiana. My mother was a tall, beautiful woman. My great-grandmother was from the Congo. She was real, real black. She was mahogany black. Her name was Idai Batiste. I knew my grandmother very well, but I just barely knew a little bit about my great-grandmother before she died, though we all are long livers. I'm seventy-one; my brother's seventy-three, and my mother is ninety-four. I have three aunties who are living and they all are past seventy.

After the world war, when my uncle and all of them came back, they had pictures made of themselves because they were all fixing to kind of scatter throughout America. The majority of them went to the West Coast. I had pictures of mother and my aunties, and pictures of my uncle, and we had a picture of my grandmother and grandfather. They were what you call middle-class people. Very few of them worked for others. They always had their own business. It makes you live on the edge all the time. You have to keep yourself together in order to compete. It's a very, very competitive world.

My grandfather bred mules, and they worked on the levee. He also hauled rice for different people because he had a wagon and a mule to get out there in the field. The mule could pull the wagon after it was filled with rice. My grandfather was a very strong, disciplined type of person. He always worked for himself.

In Dayton, Texas, my uncle started working at the Southern Pacific railroad, and soon after that my father and another uncle got jobs there too. My parents were Delphina and Paul Provost.

My first encounter with a commercial photographer was when I was a little boy. I was between eight and twelve. I'm Catholic, and when we made our first communion, we had a photographer come and take the group picture. There were about thirty-five or forty of us who made our first communion. We were all dressed up: the girls in white with white veils and the boys with black suits, white shirts, and black ties. Everyone had prayer books and prayer beads.

My mother wanted the pictures to send back to her people in Louisiana, and the man charged her a dollar and a half for the pictures. The photographer was Mr. A. C. Teal, and that dollar and a half was almost as much as my daddy made all day long working. And I looked at that photographer collecting the money and it just stayed with me. He came in a car. I think it was a Pierce-Arrow, and in one day he made more money than my daddy made all year working. God works in mysterious ways, because when I went into the service I was able to meet this very kind fellow who taught me some things about photography.

Teal was an advanced photographer. He was very advanced. He was not a picture-taker. He was a real professional photographer. He made group pictures of graduation classes for universities and colleges. He went all over Texas, and I think even to Alabama and Florida.

Years later I studied under Teal, and I got to be a friend of his. And there were lots of things that I learned from him. First of all, I learned how to canvas Texas. Through his teaching I went from one school to another. And I learned how to upgrade a school. We started a school with fifty cents a student, giving them a picture, a couple of pictures, and then three or four years later, we got them paying a dollar and a half, two dollars a picture. You can't go in a school at the very beginning, like those little schools in Nacogdoches, Henderson, and places like that, and ask for top dollars for your picture. I'm talking about 1947–48–49; you couldn't ask for that kind of money for pictures.

I studied with Teal while I was at Texas Southern University. He had a school of photography there, but the unique thing about it, he was not an employee at Texas Southern. He was a very self-sufficient person.

Benny Joseph was another photographer who studied with Teal. He worked with me after I opened my studio in 1949, and worked on a commission basis. He had another full-time job, and did photography part-time and then got into it real strong.

There was a time, especially around 1949–50–51–52, that there few top-notch black photographers. I came to Houston when I was real qualified, because I had the background at a top-notch portrait school in New Haven.

Louise Martin was working in Houston at that time and she was a socialite photographer. She was working on art, art-like photography. She wanted to do oil painting. That was the popular thing to do because it was not done in a natural color.

I still do some of that kind of work, but we do it on canvas. She was doing it on fiber-based prints. I can't really say too much about Ms. Martin. We spoke from a business standpoint when we saw each other. The occasions were few, but other than that I stayed too busy.

I did school photography. We would leave here in Houston and go down to Highway 59. We touched eighteen schools between Houston and Texarkana. We would service eighteen schools. And then we would come back and we would go down Highway 98, and we would touch about eight schools between Houston and Beaumont. We did schools in Orange, Port Arthur, Galveston, and other places. We were a team of photographers. There were three of us.

I had Frank Lawrence Turner. He was a graphic consultant who published yearbooks and handled class rings, invitations, and he booked the junior and senior prom. That was his area, and he stayed busy all the time. All I did was shoot, and then there was also my wife, Georgia. Her maiden name was Doyle. I taught her to take photographs about ten or twelve years ago, and she turned out to be a top-notch photographer. She could handle children. She took courses in psychology. There's an art to photographing children.

I started off with a Speed Graphic, and then went to a Leica, and later we were introduced to a 70mm camera for school work. I used to use an old Elwood enlarger, and a Besseler and an Omega. We used Opal G paper. We found out that it had an olive tone and it would not give us black black. That was the secret that we had; we always were able to get tone in our

Herbert Provost, *Self-Portrait*, Houston, Texas, 1965.

pictures instead of a white white and a black black. We also did a terrific amount of hand-tinting and sepia toning. We used to call it gold tone.

In 1963 or '64 we began shooting color, and we found a place that could process our color work for us and give it to us in a package deal. It made a big difference, but I didn't know it would break me. The company that did the manufacturing was the one that made the money, because his money was guaranteed. We had to get out there and sell the contracts, service the contract, and then beg to get the money. Then all the pictures that they don't pick up, you have to eat them. The company gave no credit for them. With black-and-white, we were the manufacturer. I didn't realize that. In fact, we didn't have the kind of expertise that it takes to run a business to really make it survive and grow.

I made the mistake of putting the schools up to about 85 percent of my work. The rest of it divided between homecomings, coronations,

and the like. I also used to photograph teas. I had observed over a period of time that the Houston community had been developed in part from people having teas on Sunday evenings around their churches and homes. We would come and photograph the ladies because they all wore their evening dress and gloves and it was a big occasion. The teas gave them a chance to dress and to visit other people's homes. People put an emphasis on their home and their home lifestyle. Sometimes we'd put pictures of them in the newspaper, talk about their organization, how old it was and how it was founded, and the installation of new officers.

I didn't work for any paper. I did assignments for papers, and I covered assignments. I had pictures at the paper so that the paper could use it. I knew all the editors and the publishers. I did work for the Houston *Informer* and the *Forward Times.*

During the years of integration, we had some problems. We had just reached a point that we had built an organizational structure. We had a department in the high schools with access to come and talk to the seniors and tell them about business. They used us as role models, and we were very professional. We had good equipment; we had good cars; we dressed with real quality; and everybody on the staff was knowledgeable and knew just exactly what we were doing and knew how to handle all the customers. We made the high school seniors feel important, and there was no competition. Nobody could run up and compete against us. They tried, but they wouldn't last. We understood the market, and we had the kind of equipment it takes to produce a quality picture. We had staff and we had the backup force.

During integration, white photographers understood what kind of money we had raised photography to in the black market. Before, they didn't bother the black market because there was still the impression that pictures were fifty cents and a dollar, but we had raised the market up to a good comfortable price.

We started off with an eight-dollar package and that was real good money for a package. But our overhead was so high because we had to stay in good hotels and eat good food and entertain ourself in the evening, you know, quality-wise, because it was a grueling thing, photographing children all day long. We would do 350 to 500 students and be through by about two o'clock that day.

I did quite a bit of work for the NAACP for a while. I was the official photographer for a while. We made civil rights cases, you know, where people got beat up. They brought them to us and we would photograph them. We had three or four people shot or beat up. I had to hide those photographs, because several times the sheriff's department came by and went through all my negatives looking for them. I told them I gave them to the NAACP. I never did keep anything. They were the ones getting them developed. They came by three or four different times, and one of them told me to be careful about what I was getting into, what I was doing. I told them, "There ain't no way in hell you can be any more of a deterrent than the Japs had been. If you were in World War II, it would be a hard thing to forget what the Japs did to people. I suffered so much. I was in a lifeboat for thirteen and a half days."

When I first went in the service I went to Norfolk, Virginia, and from Norfolk I went to the U.S.S. *Arkansas,* then to the U.S.S. *A.P.838,* an attack transport. Then I went aboard the *Quincy*; that was a cruiser, and then on an A.P.858 and that was where we got sunk. I got off with twenty-six other people. We had two lifeboats and we stayed thirteen and a half days on it. It was a hell of an experience.

The service at that time was segregated. One set of pictures I did for the NAACP was at the bus station downtown where they had the white people going in for service. They were eating in the front part of the bus station where the cafeteria was, and the black soldiers were eating in the kitchen. I photographed it and before I got to my place, a policeman was there outside waiting for me, but I'd already gotten rid of the film.

I've had studios in Houston in different locations. The first one was at Dowling and Gray Streets. I was there for about three years. I went to 2411 Dowling, and I stayed there about three years, and went to the corner of Dowling and Elgin. And there I learned that it was not good to have a crowd of people coming in and out of your place. I stayed until I learned that and moved to Wheeler Street, about a block and a half from Dowling Street, near Texas Southern

University. That was in 1964 and 1965, and in 1966 I came to my present location on South MacGregor. I live upstairs.

I used to love darkroom work. All the work I did was commercial. I didn't have time to shoot anything else. But I was also a tennis coach for twelve years, from 1966 to 1978. I taught part-time at Texas Southern. Tennis had become part of my life since the war years. I started playing when I was stationed on a French island in the Pacific. Those French officers had a country club, but then they all went back to Algeria and back to France before the war and during the war, and they left the country club. Then the Americans came to the island and made a base and they upgraded the facilities for the officers. Quite a few officers would come and spend the weekends there. They played tennis and jogged all the way to the top part of the mountain. It wasn't too high, but it was high enough. I was then a steward first class, and they put me in charge of the whole complex, and I learned to play tennis by watching the officers. Then, when one of the officers didn't show up, the one that was there wanted me to hit the ball with him. I was an athlete. So it wasn't too much trouble for me.

After I got out of the service, I did lots of competing. I used to travel all over the East Coast playing those tournaments up there in the American Tennis Association. I even played Arthur Ashe's teacher. His name was Dr. Johnson. He was a hell of a player. He had a good drop shot, but I was so young and so strong that his drop shot didn't work. I never did show my age.

I still play most every time I get the weather break. I have somebody to come in and they work me out for about an hour or an hour and a half. I just get worked out, that's all. I doubt if I could play a good strong competition game now. I couldn't concentrate that long.

I never did photograph tennis. When I'm at a tennis match, I'm watching one of my players. So I never did get off into making their pictures. But I did lots of photographs of other community groups. I was the official photographer for Local 872, the longshoremen's union, and also for the Antioch Baptist Church. I didn't do much work for the Catholic churches because I was out of the range of what they were paying.

I never did much work for the black

sororities. They generally had their affairs on Saturdays and on Friday nights. Well, on Friday, we'd be coming off the highway, and we didn't need it. I did do some work for Don Robey. They would send their orders to my studio to be photographed. I photographed Bobby "Blue" Bland and Ray Charles, but I can't put my hands on those negatives.

When I had my studio at the corner of Dowling and Elgin, they had the Eldorado Social Club upstairs, and they would have dances. But I never would go there because they had a photographer who would do that. We did studio portrait work. We knew how to relax peo-

ple. We're called Provost and Associates now, but up until about fifteen years ago we were the Provost Trio. My son, Jerome, is starting to get involved in the business now. He's a top-notch photographer. He's twenty-six. He learned it. It's just part of him, and he knows it.

I haven't retired. I can't retire. What would I do? It's a unique business because it reflects the individual. I possess a ball of energy. And if somebody comes up with an idea, "Why don't we do that?" I say, "Now, what's stopping us?" You know, once you get involved, you say, "Fine." You do it; then I'm through with it.

Herbert Provost, *Our Mother of Mercy Church Confirmation*, Houston, Texas, 1958.

Herbert Provost, *Betty Baptiste (Guy), Coronation, Southern Unversity,* Baton Rouge, Lousiana, 1964.

Herbert Provost, *Seated Girl*, Houston, Texas, 1963.

Herbert Provost, *Bowling Team,* Houston, Texas, 1971.

Herbert Provost, *Students, Texas Southern University,* Houston, Texas, 1978.

Herbert Provost, *Homecoming Queen, Texas Southern University,* Houston, Texas, 1972.

Herbert Provost, *Reception at Southern University,* Baton Rouge, Louisiana, 1964.

Herbert Provost, *Southern University Band*, Baton Rouge, Louisiana, ca. 1960s.

Herbert Provost, *Nurse Graduate*, Houston, Texas, 1969.

Herbert Provost, *Coronation*, Houston, Texas, 1967.

Earlie Hudnall Jr.

I was born in Hattiesburg, Mississippi, on November 8, 1946, at 4:15 in the afternoon. I'm the eldest of six children to my father, Earlie Hudnall Sr. My mother's name is Herlene; her maiden name is Lewis. I grew up and was educated through high school in Hattiesburg.

My interest in photography grew out of my grandmother, my father's mother, Bonnie Jean Reed, telling us old stories about how things used to be. She had kept a photo album of my father's pictures when he was in the service and of community people, community events, and all these kinds of things.

On the fourth Sunday after church, my father would make pictures of us. And he made pictures as we grew up and through various stages of life: first day of school, elementary school, special birthdays and these kinds of things. My grandmother was a family and community historian. She kept everything: obituaries, when people died, when people did this, the time I went to the hospital and my mother had an operation, when my father had an appendicitis operation. She kept up with everything going on through life.

She used to sit on the porch during the summertime and she would tell us stories about how things used to be. I found that very intriguing and at an early point in my life I learned the value of recording history.

In high school, I had an opportunity to have an experience with photography. Our physics instructor was showing us the difference between a chemical change and a physical change by using a drugstore negative and a light box. One thousand and one, one thousand and two, into the developer for one minute, into the fix for one minute, turn on the light, and wow, we had a creation. For me, that stuck.

I never intended to become a photographer. Early on I had wanted to become a doctor because in the first grade, my teacher sent me to the office to get the first-aid kit. I walked through the door and she said, "Wow, here comes Doctor Hudnall." So up until about the fifth or sixth grade, my intentions were to become a doctor. But at that time, I decided I wanted to become an artist because I had an opportunity to work on decorating a homecoming float. And we won first place that year. So all of my attention went toward art.

In high school, after processing those drugstore negatives, I used to use my father's camera. I went into the room, took his camera that he hung on the wall on a nail above the door, and one summer while making photographs, I dropped the camera into the swimming pool at a city park. I got it out, dried it off, took the camera and hid it in the attic. No one ever knew what happened to the camera and my father completely forgot about it after that. Years later, we talked about it, and my father said that he had purchased it in 1942 in Joliet, Illinois. It was a box camera, and it might still be in the attic today; I need to check.

After joining the Marine Corps, while I was in basic training and advanced infantry training at Camp Pendleton in California, I purchased a little Kodak Instamatic camera and used to make photographs with that. Mainly, I made pictures because I remembered the ones that my grandmother had in the album that my father had made while he was in service. And as a son who wanted to be like his father, I began to make pictures of activities and things that we were involved in, maneuvers in the fields and these kinds of things. For me, composition became very, very important. It was almost like second nature. I didn't have any problem with composition. My pictures were clear, and all the way through Vietnam, when time permitted, I shot pictures. I still have some slides today. Composition came very natural.

In the fall of 1968, I came out of the service and entered Texas Southern University as an art major under the tutelage of Dr. John Biggers, who was the head of the art department. On the first day of our freshman orientation, he told us, "Art is life; it's life that evolves around you and these are the things that you should be involved in and that you should show in your work." And from that day until this, that philosophy has stuck with me.

In our first drawing class, we had to do a study from nature and I chose to do a photograph and work from that. I learned that there was a darkroom in the art department, and I asked Dr. Biggers if it was okay for me to use it and he said yes. It so happened that it was June 19, 1969, and the university students were celebrating Juneteenth in Texas. It was always the big festival on campus, when we had watermelons that came from Hempstead. And during that particular day I met a guy named Nathaniel Sweets. He was a photography major from St. Louis, where his father was a newspaper publisher. I said, "Well, hey, I have a camera in my room," and he said, "If you shoot some pictures, we can develop them in the darkroom and I can print them in the photolab in Mr. Evans's class."

I said, "Okay," and I shot pictures on that particular day and Nathaniel Sweets and I became friends. But we found out that it was impossible for us to use the darkroom in the photolab after hours and instead we used the one in the art department. In the darkroom Nathaniel familiarized me with the enlarger and taught me how it worked. It was like a new breath of life, and from that day on, I've been on my own. So, in essence, I'm a self-taught photographer.

After working that way for some period of time, I began to enroll in photographic classes at the university under Mr. Evans. I was an art major at the time, but my interests lay more toward photography and I devoted more toward photography, less time toward art. Then I began to get requests from students across campus. I shot everything that I possibly could. I shot baseball games if I could get there; I shot

Earlie Hudnall Jr., *Self-Portrait*, Houston, Texas, ca. 1980s.

coeds on campus; I shot organizations; I shot people's sculptures in the art department. The art department stayed open until eleven and twelve at night. I would be over there shooting people's models for their pieces and so forth, and lo and behold this little Fuji camera that I had purchased while I was in Vietnam at the PX in Danang, Southeast Asia, I dropped it. My camera was broken and my life was somewhat shattered. A friend of mine, named Alvin McEwing (who finished TSU with a degree in industrial arts with an emphasis in photography), had a Yashicamat 124G twin-lens camera, and he gave it to me to use. So, at that point, I was introduced to the 2¼ format that I'm very partial to. And for about the next five or six years, that was all I used. And a lot of my work today that I'm still printing from those negatives are on the Yashicamat 124G.

Also, in 1969 at Texas Southern, I had an opportunity to start working on student publications with Ray Carrington, who now is a excellent friend of mine. At that time, he was the yearbook editor and he needed some photographs to finish out the student life section. Someone had told him about me and said, "There's a guy on campus named Hudnall who's an art major, and man, he has pictures of a little bit of everything."

So Ray came over to the art department to seek me out. He said, "Hey, man, I heard that you have some photographs."

I said, "Yeah, I have a few," and he said, "Well, let me see. I could use these in my yearbook." And giving Ray those particular photographs has led to a lifelong relationship for the past twenty-five years. We have worked together on several projects.

I became the yearbook editor three years after we met, in 1973 to be exact, and Ray and I worked very closely with the students. The yearbook gave me an opportunity in my formative years to photograph on the campus at Texas Southern University through trial and error, and to also photograph in the community around the university. Up until this time, from about 1968 to 1972, my whole world revolved on the campus. I lived on the campus, and from sunup to sundown I was in the art department. I was in the photolab. I was somewhere on campus shooting an event and at each event it seemed to be exciting because there were people there.

When I was a senior in the art department, I had to paint a mural which I had started in my junior year. I was working on a mural sketch on a wall in Hanna Hall, where there were murals that were painted by senior art students as a part of this requirement for graduation. I was trying to get an early start and so, at this point I was working on the wall.

Dr. Thomas Freeman, the debate coach at TSU, walked up to me one day, and said, "Are you Earlie Hudnall?"

I said, "Yes, sir," and he said, "Well, I need to talk to you in my office. Are you a photographer?"

I said, "Yes, sir," and he asked, "How would you like to work for me on the weekend?" So, I went over to his office and he told me that Mr. Evans had referred me to him. He wanted me to do some photographs of the activities of the continuing education people who met on Tuesday and Thursday nights. I've forgotten exactly how much he told me the pay would be, but it was exciting because here was an opportunity to do other photographs. From seven to nine in the evening I did classroom shots and sometimes guest speakers, and so forth and so on.

My buddy, Ray Carrington, was also working there as a photographer. Well, Dr. Freeman loved the photographs; he loved the expression, and he loved the detail and everything. This also gave me an opportunity to start getting off campus into the Houston community. He wanted me to go to the community centers to show how people lived and what they did from day to day. This opened my eyes to a whole new world. But there was also something that was familiar to me. There were people that I saw that reminded me of home—their mannerisms, the community life, greeting people, speaking to people, elderly people, young people. For me, there was a continuity of life that was recycling that went over and over and over again. This was something that was very important to me. It touched upon the same principles and philosophies that I was brought up to believe, the same things that my grandmother talked about and showed me in the photo album. Here was an opportunity for me to capture a lot of these things. And from then on, this has been my basic approach to photography, to document things around us. Cities and famous dates seem important, but the lives of people from day to day are also important—how we dress on Sundays, how we dress during the week, where we go, what we do for entertainment, how we look. This is what my work has all been about.

Another person who influenced me was Herbert Provost. I met Mr. Provost in about 1970. He had a studio at the corner of Dowling and Elgin Streets underneath the Eldorado ballroom. And Mr. Provost had been a photographer here in Houston since about 1950, if I'm correct, after he left the service. He was in the navy for a number of years, and he opened up a studio here in Houston. Coach Provost, as I will call him or refer to him, or "Pro," as we formerly called him. He was the tennis coach at Texas Southern University from about 1970 up until the early '80s. And during that particular time Ray Carrington, who was a tennis player for Corpus Christi, Texas, was also the yearbook editor.

Well, Mr. Provost was a photographer as well as a tennis player. He also sold yearbooks and represented the Intercollegiate Press out of Kansas City, Kansas. So he would bid all the yearbook contracts at Texas Southern, Prairie View, Wiley College, and most of the other predominantly black schools in Texas and Louisiana. And Provost won the contract at Texas Southern for a number of years. So we had to work together: Mr. Provost as the company representative, Mr. Evans as the university photographer, and Ray Carrington and myself as student photographers. It gave us the opportunity to have a dialogue.

Mr. Provost wanted us to produce a good book, and he would always come in and critique our photographs, teach us things about lighting, or make comments about lighting, and how things should be and how we should do it and so forth. Well, one summer I wanted to go home. I had a car and I needed some brake shoes for the car. So Mr. Provost said, "I'll get your brake shoes for you, but what I want you to do is to tear out a floor in my darkroom for me so that I can have it resurfaced."

I said, "Fine, I'll be happy to do that." I was excited about getting my car fixed. I could go home during the school break.

Mr. Provost took me to the auto mechanic repair store on Dowling and purchased the brake shoes and put them in my hand and I said, "Pro, how am I going to put them on?"

He said, "Hey, do it yourself."

What I ended up doing was taking down both sides, leaving one side attached so I could see how things went back together. And I put the brake shoes on and they worked. Then Pro said, "See, you can do anything that you want to do if you just try."

So, through that association, I began to hang around him. At that time he knew Muhammad Ali; he knew another guy in the city named Lloyd Wells who was a scout for the Kansas City Chiefs. They always had famous stories to tell about things. They always were around celebrities at that particular time.

Provost's wife, Georgia Provost, used to run the photo studio. And after I did the menial tasks and he saw that I could shoot pictures, Provost said, "Hey, I want you to do this picture."

"Pro, I don't think that I can do it."

"Well, hey, just go ahead and try, use the studio." And he basically turned the studio over to us. We had full reins of the studio and full reins of the darkroom. Facilities were limited on campus and I ended up spending a lot of time with Provost—in the evenings, after school, every day, on the weekend, sleeping at the studio. He had bunkbeds there, so we slept there. Photography became second nature. We were there all the time.

Mainly, we did portraits, school-day pictures, group photographs, social events, and weddings. And whenever we would shoot, Pro would always have a critique. "Your lighting should have been this way; your lighting should be that way, you should do it this way—Rembrandt lighting, side lighting, the north light, how important it was, how important it was to shoot at f11 at 500 with the flash in. Use your field flash when you're doing your group shots on the outside—how to arrange large groups; how to put lighter people in the background, darker people up front. If you're shooting group shots, separate your colors, don't put people in white next to white, if you do, you got to use a field card."

So we went the whole gamut of what was going on. And to this day, Pro is the same way. He stresses lighting, lighting, and lighting. Through that, Ray and I had an opportunity to work over a number of years on numerous projects with Mr. Provost. I considered his tutelage invaluable to my career as a photographer. As a matter of fact, there were several people, but Pro was very instrumental in the early years of my career in photography.

I learned to retouch negatives from Provost. Mrs. Provost was very good at retouching and she used to retouch just about all of the negatives late at night. Early on, Pro used to make mention of changing skin highlights. But at the time that I came aboard or was around him, they had large contracts for high schools. So they were developing long, large reels of black-and-white film and making contact sheets and contact prints, 200 to 300 or 400 to 500 a night. They had to get out the work for three or four schools in a week's time. It was like an assembly line. They would print the pictures black-and-white, wash them, tone them, lay them out, let them dry. Then they would mix the colors and go back and hand tint the lips or just put a little highlight on the face for the rouge and so forth and just a little bit of color. That's the way my high school graduation picture was made. And it was called a color photograph at that time, an 8x10. Pro had two or three people working with him and they would do all these orders. And on the weekend, they would go back to those small towns and drop off the prints. They might be gone two or three days and come back with $400 to $800. That was a lot of money to make in a week's time.

In school I was taught to use what they called a little grease from the forehead or whatever on the lens in a certain kind of way so it gives a little highlight. And early on, I was able to make some very interesting portraits that way. It softens the light using that technique. And in the darkroom I used almost anything that light would shine through, such as a stocking, a piece of cellophane, a piece of plastic, or whatever to diffuse the light to soften the photograph. It added something different to the picture. Sometimes I'd burn in the edges on the photograph, but now I prefer to present it to you as it is because that's the only way I think there's beauty. You don't have to alter anything in the scene. I may crop it and I may burn it in a little bit more to put emphasis upon what I want. But now, I'd never go back and etch a photograph or burn something in or take it completely out. That's not me. That's not my style.

Mr. Provost made me conscious of how to pose a group picture, but in my own work I tend to allow it to happen before the camera. And at that moment I ask myself, "Is this what I want?" If it's not, I kind of move, I try not to direct my subjects as much as I possibly can, but in doing a group shot, it comes back. I hear Provost in the back of my mind talking about lighting and about how to pose a group and how to arrange a group.

I think that photography has a different place in people's lives today than it did when Provost was most active as a photographer. Back then, it was more of a luxury. Now, cameras are more available. Anyone can pick up an Instamatic camera.

The film and printing papers are different today. Ninety-five percent of the time I use the

TMAX films, 400 ASA and 100 ASA, though mostly 400 ASA. Early on, I used to use TriX 400 for my black-and-white work. For paper, I'm using Ilford and have for the last twenty years, either the Ilford Gallery, or multigrade fiber-based papers. Generally, I use two fixing baths now and do selenium toning.

For me, the main thing is to be conscious of what is going on and to understand the importance there is to document it. Back then people might have questioned me as to why I want to photograph what I do. "Why not wait until I put on my Sunday best and my finery of things to pose for a picture?" But I like to capture a person as he or she is from day to day—how they work, how they actually live, so that we can better understand their condition.

We tend to bring out the finest and the best when the guests come. But I like to show it all, as it really is, and I think that fifty years ago, people would question it, more so than today, though even today people question it. "Why are you here? Why are you making that photograph?" And I have to use my own personal touch and my own personal way of answering that question in my approach to photography.

Photography then was making a living. This was their profession and this is what they did from day to day in order to live. People came into the studio. That's the good part of the photography that Mr. Provost, Ms. Martin, and Mr. Joseph captured during those years. But there's also a tragedy about it, especially from the standpoint that you rarely see the common everyday people who went to work, who rode the bus, who walked the street, who traveled back and forth by foot. Instead, you see the people who would dress up and go to the studio to have their picture made—the ones who could afford it. They wanted to look their very best because it was a portrait of them. This is how they wanted to be seen.

Mr. Provost had a very specific kind of approach. He had an assignment to go and do, and it was accomplished that way: an address, a group shot, or wedding, something that was specific. My approach comes from basic instinct and from my identification with the community. I'm always aware of what is going on around me. I'm very conscious of what is happening and of the simple things—the way a child may sit, the way an old man may look, the way in which a house may be situated, or a certain particular building in the community that has been a cornerstone, or has been in the community a long time. For me, I work out of a love. Pro worked primarily for a financial reward, but he was meticulous in doing the job right and being sure that he got the most out of his group. I use somewhat of an open approach and I take advantage of an opportunity that presents itself as I walk and travel through the community. It's more like reminiscing for me, and seeing what happens. I feel that I have to be on the scene. I have to be in the community in order to make a good picture.

Earlie Hudnall Jr., *Mother with Sons,* Houston, Texas, 1973. *Courtesy Benteler-Morgan Galleries.*

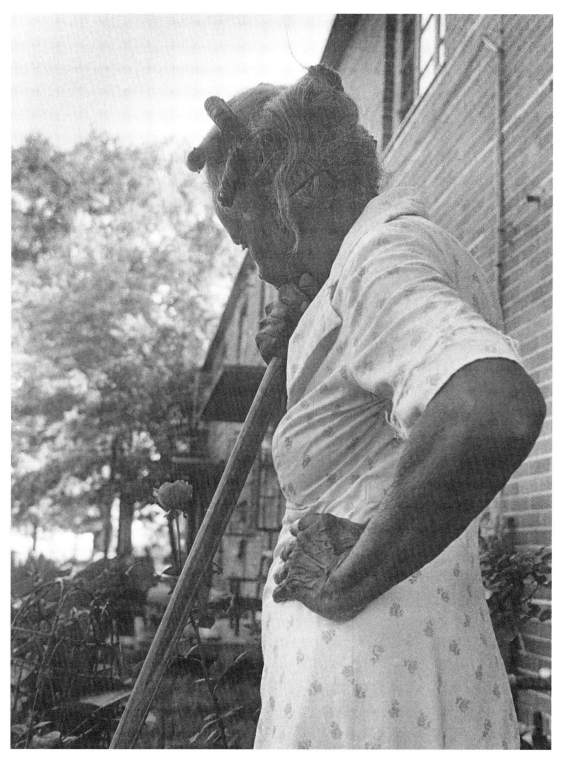

Earlie Hudnall Jr., *My Thinking Time*, Houston, Texas, 1980. *Courtesy Benteler-Morgan Galleries.*

Earlie Hudnall Jr., *Red Rose Inn*, Houston, Texas, 1983. *Courtesy Benteler-Morgan Galleries.*

Earlie Hudnall Jr., *Jelly and Friends*, Houston, Texas, 1983. *Courtesy Benteler-Morgan Galleries.*

Earlie Hudnall Jr., *Flipping Boy*, Houston, Texas, 1983. *Courtesy Benteler-Morgan Galleries.*

Earlie Hudnall Jr., *Lady with Flag, July 4th*, Houston, Texas, 1987. *Courtesy Benteler-Morgan Galleries.*

Earlie Hudnall Jr., *Lady in Plaid Skirt*, Houston, Texas, 1990. *Courtesy Benteler-Morgan Galleries.*

Earlie Hudnall Jr., *Lady in Black Hat with Feathers*, Houston, Texas, 1990. *Courtesy Benteler-Morgan Galleries.*

Earlie Hudnall Jr., *Cowboy,* Houston, Texas, 1993. *Courtesy Benteler-Morgan Galleries.*

Earlie Hudnall Jr., *Hip Hop*, Galveston, Texas, 1994. *Courtesy Benteler-Morgan Galleries.*

APPENDIX I

Selected Listing of African American Photographers in Texas, 1866–1994

AUSTIN

Morris Crawford (1920–1983)	1950s–1983	3515 East Martin Luther King Jr. Blvd.
Robert Ross	1930s–1950s	900 East 11th Street, official photographer for Austin *Negro Life* in 1950–1951
Robert Whitby (1914–1978)	1950s–1978	1808 Wildrose Drive

DALLAS

A. B. Bell (1913–1989)	1947–1976	Freelance photographer, Dallas *Post Tribune*, Dallas *Express* Bishop College/Dallas
	1977–1979	Studio on Elm Street
	1979–1987	1435 East Red Bird Lane
Marion Butts (1924–)	1947–1948	3504 Munger
	1954	2604 Thomas (Dallas *Express*)
	1962–1975	Corner of Oakland and Carpenter Freeway
	1988	1412 Bonnieview
Cato Brown	1947–1948	Cato's Studio, 2306 Hall Street
Noel P. Brown	1941–1942	2700 Flora
M. S. Dunlavy	1941–1942	3619 Havana
Alex Galloway	1941–1942	2813 Thomas
R. C. Hickman (1922–)	1949–1961	Freelance photographer, Dallas *Star Post*, NAACP, *Jet* Magazine
Dewitt Humphrey (1917–1980)	1930s	Hall Street
	1940s	Allen Street
	1948–1954?	2715 Bryan
	1960s	2327 Dathe Street
	1970s–1980	Oakland Avenue
George Keaton (1933–)	1951	Anderson Studio on Oakland Avenue
	1965–1979	2700 block of Grand
	1980–	1916 Martin Luther King Blvd.

This listing was gathered from interviews, census records, and city directories around Texas, and is not definitive of the history of the entire state.

Carl Sidle (1943–)	1971–	204 Conrad Street
Rev. Walter I. Solomon	1941–1942	New York Studio, 2212 Hall
	1944–1946	3204 Thomas
Taft Wilson	1947–1948	3408 San Jacinto
Emma King Woodard	1941–1948	Woodard's Studio, 3415 Howell

FORT WORTH

Calvin Littlejohn (1909–1993)	1934	Ninth Street
		901 East Harvey
	1947–1950	1057 Evans
	1950–1952	826 Missouri
	1952–1962	1057 Evans
	1962–1993	901 East Harvey

GALVESTON

Albert Beverly (1891–?)	1900	
Ardell Beverly (1877–?)	1900	
Willie Christian (1879–?)	1900	
Lucius Harper	1890–91	Winnie, 33rd & 34th
(listed as artist in city directory)	1896–97	2907 Avenue M ½
	1899–1902	1303 29th
John E. Palmer (1891–1964)		
Joe Thompson (1865–?)		

HARRISON COUNTY

Larry Rogers	1900	

HOUSTON

Nicholas Broussard	1908–1909	1019 Tuam (restaurant owner)
	1910–1911	1019 Tuam (restaurant owner)
	1911–1912	1019 Vine (photographer)
	1912–1915	1910 St. Emanuel (photographer)
	1916	3417 Stonewall (photographer)
	1918	1619 Brewster (photographer)
	1919	3102 Dennis (no occupation listed)
	1920–1924	3102 Dennis (photographer)
	1925–1929	2412 Calhoun (photographer)

Randolph Brown	1908–1909	704 House (picture enlarger)
	1910–1911	2819 Nance (proprietor, Big Tree Photo and Enlarging House, Photographer, Picture Enlarger)
	1911–1912	630 San Felipe (photographer)
	1912	612 Robin (photographer/picture enlarger)
Rodney Evans (1922–)	1952–1991	Instructor, Texas Southern University
Seth Fitch	1920–1921	2004 Austin (chauffeur)
	1922	911 Milam (studio address)
	1923–1924	no entry
	1925	5000 Montrose Blvd. (chauffeur)
Elnora Frazier (1924–)	1942–1955	Worked for Teal Studio
	1955–1989	Worked for Courtesy Photo; Floyd Photo; National Photographic Lab
Lucius Harper	1905–1907	1107 Andrews
Charles G. Harris	1903–1909	Little Rock, Arkansas
	1909–1931	811 San Felipe (later changed to West Dallas Avenue)
	1941	309 Polk Avenue
	1943–1944	811 W. Dallas
Earlie Hudnall Jr. (1946–)	1973	University Photographer, TSU
	1976	B.A., Texas Southern University, Art Education
Benny Joseph (1924–)	1950–1953	Worked for Herbert Provost
	1958–1968	3505A Wheeler
	1968–1982	2305 Blodgett (studio)
	1982–	3608 Rio Vista
Gertrude Lewis	1917	2318½ Dowling (no occupation listed)
	1918	2307½ Dowling (hairdresser)
	1919	no listing
	1922–1924	2307 Dowling (music teacher)
	1925	2307 Dowling (photographer)
	1926	2307 Dowling (music teacher)
Louise Martin (1911–1995)	1946–1956	2008 Maury
	1957–1962	2902 Rosedale
	1963–	3008 Wichita
		4200 block of Dowling
Ivery Myers (1919–)	1943	Prairie View, worked for Teal Studio
	1944–1945	1066 Sycamore Street, Teal Studio, San Antonio

	1945–1946	New Orleans *Sentinel,* New Orleans, Louisiana
	1947	Moved to Houston
Herbert Provost (1921–)	1949–1952	1806 Dowling
	1952–1955	2411 Dowling
	1955–1964	Corner of Dowling and Elgin (downstairs from Eldorado Ballroom)
Edward M. Robinson	1907	407 ½ Travis (proprietor of Eureka Studio, photographer)
	1908–1909	no listing
	1910–1911	2816 Cline (laborer for Cleveland Compress)
	1912–1915	409 Schwartz (laborer)
Arthur Chester Teal (1891?–1956)	1919	1111 Andrew (commercial photographer)
	1920–1921	620 W. Dallas (photographer)
	1922	no listing
	1923–1924	620 W. Dallas (no occupation listed)
	1925	307 W. Dallas (Teal Studio)
	1926	2420 Dowling
	1926–1927	409 ½ Milam
	1927	4203 Lyons (5th Ward) (residence)
	1928	409 ½ Milam (Studio #1)
		224 Pilgrim Bldg. (Studio #2)
	1929	221–224 Pilgrim Bldg. (#1)
		409 ½ Milam (#2)
	1930–1935	2218 Brackenridge (residence)
	1930–1933	219–224 Pilgrim Bldg.(#1)
		409 ½ Milam (#2)
	1934–1941	500 Louisiana (Odd Fellows building)
	1943–1944	2112 ½ and 2320 Dowling
	1943–1944	3308 Lyons
	1956	2301 Jensen Drive
E. W. Teal Residence	1959	3206 ½ Lyons
Teal Studio	1959	2218 Brackenridge
Teal Studio	1963	3206 ½ Lyons
Teal Studio (commercial) Elmon P. Gray	1963	2709 Campbell
Teal Studio	1965	3206 ½ Lyons
Teal Studio Elmon P. Gray	1965	2820 Brackenridge
Joe Thomas	1900	

Mary Warren	1866	Main Street (photographic printer)
Lloyd Wells	1953–1954	1806 Dowling
	1955–1965	2316 Elgin
Juanita Williams (1926–)	1941–1952	Worked for Teal Studio
	1954–1962	Worked part-time for Courtesy Photo; Herbert Provost; Benny Joseph
	1962–	5125 Reed Road

JASPER

Alonzo W. Jordan (1903–1984)

LUBBOCK

Robert O'Neal (1952–)

Eugene Roquemore (1921–1993)

MARSHALL

Rudolph L. Beaver (1915–)

Fred Weathersby Sr. (1919–)

PEARSALL

Thomas Banks (b. 1865)	1900	

TEXARKANA

R. C. McClendon (1926–)

Barbara Pitts (1959–)

TYLER

Curtis Humphrey (1907–1996)	1932	Harry Berkman and Harry Garonzik Studio, Fort Worth
	1930s–1942	Thomas and Hall, Dallas
	1946	Wiley College, Marshall
	1947	Texas College, Tyler
	1954–	2205 North Grand, Tyler

APPENDIX II

Selected Listing of African American Newspapers and Magazines in Texas*

African Herald. 1992–. Monthly. Publisher: Richard O. Nwachukwu. Editor: Richard O. Nwachukwu. Dallas.

Applause: The Magazine of Inspiration. 1946–?. Frequency unknown. Publisher: Don Gilbert. Editor: Don Gilbert. Dallas.

Association of Black Sociologists Newsletter. 1974?–?. Frequency unknown. Publisher: Association of Black Sociologists. Editor: Florence Bonner. Houston.

Austin *Informer.* 1905?–?. Weekly. Austin.

Austin *Mirror.* 1958–?. Weekly. Publisher: Walter McBride. Editor: Dora H. Moore. Austin.

Austin *Searchlight.* 1986?–?. Weekly. Publisher: William Mabson. Editor: William P. Mabson. Austin.

Bishop *Herald.* 1882?–?. Six times a year. Publisher: Bishop College. Editors: C. F. Richardson, Apr. 1931; Marjorie Wilkerson, Feb. 1933. Marshall.

Black Economic Times. 1993–. Biweekly. Publisher: Chevis King Jr. Editor: Joe Howard. Dallas.

Black Revolution. 1967?–?. Biweekly. Publisher: Student Nonviolent Coordinating Committee. Houston.

Black Tie. 1990–. Bimonthly. Publisher: Henry F. Harvey III. Editor: Zelda M. Harvey. Houston.

Booker T. Informer. 1927?–?. Frequency unknown. Publisher: Students of Booker T. Washington High School. Dallas.

Bronze Texas News. 1965?–?. Weekly. Publisher: M. Wilson. Fort Worth.

Brotherhood Eyes. 1930s. Weekly. Publisher: William Sidney Pittman. Editor: William Sidney Pittman. Dallas.

Buffalo. 1980–1982. Monthly. Publisher: APA Communications. Editors: Ariel P. Wiley, Nov. 1980–May 1981; William C. Pratt, June 1981–Jan. 1982. Marshall.

The Bulletin. 1922?–?. Monthly during school year. Publisher: Samuel Huston College. Editors: Timothy B. Echols, Mar. 1925; Earl Swisher, Dec. 6, 1933; S. F. Ray, Aug. 1934; Elmo Tatum, Feb. 22, 1935; Dorothy Butler, Feb.–Mar. 1944; Johnnie Mae Johnson, Jan. 28–May 1946; B. Luis Downs, Dec. 20, 1946–Nov. 29, 1947; Frizella Whitiker, Nov. 1948. Austin.

Bulletin, Prairie View State Normal and Industrial College. 1909?–?. Quarterly. Publisher: Prairie View State Normal and Industrial College. Prairie View.

Butler Bear. 1945–?. Monthly. Publisher: Butler College. Tyler.

The Call. 1919?–. Weekly. Publisher: C. A. Franklin. Houston.

The Call (Texas edition). 1929?–?. Publisher: C. A. Franklin. Houston.

Campus Defender. 1992–. Bimonthly. Publisher: Sonceria Messiah. Editor: ReShonda L. Tate. Houston.

Capital City Argus. 1962–1969. Weekly. Publisher: Arthur Sims. Austin.

Capital City Argus. 1971–198?. Weekly. Publisher: Arthur Sims. Austin.

Capital City Argus and Interracial Review. 1969–1971. Weekly. Publisher: Mason Smith. Austin.

Cen-Tex Reflections: The Citizen Newspaper. 1984–?. Weekly. Waco.

City Times. 1898?–?. Weekly. Publisher: City Times Publishing Company. Editor: William H. Noble Jr. Galveston.

The Conservative Counselor. 1909?–?. Weekly. Gonzales.

Corpus Christi *Weekly.* 1960?–?. Weekly. Publisher: Corpus Christi Publishing Company. Editor: Reynell Parkins. Corpus Christi.

Dallas *Examiner.* 1986–. Weekly. Publisher: Fred Finch Jr. Editor: Jeffrey Douglas, Apr.

---

* This listing of African American newspapers and magazines has been compiled from a variety of sources, including existing bibliographic records, business directories, and interviews. In some instances, the dates given indicate available volumes and not inclusive dates of publication.

23, 1986–June 4, 1986. Dallas.

Dallas *Express.* 1893–?. Weekly. Publisher: Carter Wesley. Editors: W. E. King, Jan. 13, 1900–Aug. 16, 1919; W. H. Pace, Sept. 22, 1934–Apr. 4, 1938; Maynard H. Jackson, Aug. 6, 1938–Mar. 9, 1940; J. Alston Atkins, Nov. 26, 1960–Oct. 6, 1962. Dallas.

Dallas *Gazette.* 1912?–?. Weekly. Publisher: J. H. Owens and Company. Editor: J. H. Owens. Dallas.

Dallas *Post Tribune.* 1947–. Weekly. Publishers: Bert Muse, Dickie Foster, and T. R. Lee. Editor: T. R. Lee. Dallas.

Dallas *Weekly.* 1954–1985. Weekly. Publisher: Anthony T. Davis. Dallas.

Dallas *Weekly.* 1985–. Weekly. Publisher: James A. Washington. Editors: Yolanda Adams, 1990–1993; Don Robinson, 1993–1995; Calvin Carter, 1995–.

Dallas *Star Post.* 1950?–196?. Weekly. Dallas. Continues as Dallas *Post Tribune.*

The Enlightener. 1968?–?. Quarterly. Publisher: St. John Baptist Church. Editor: Thelma L. Wells. Dallas.

Examiner. 1940?–1941. Weekly. Publisher: Bertron M. Jackson. Galveston. Continues as Galveston *Examiner.*

Exodus III: African American Family History Journal. 1992–. Quarterly. Publisher: Exodus III Publications. Editor: Kevin Hendrick. Austin.

Fort Worth *Eagle Eye.* 1934?–?. Weekly. Publisher: P. R. Register. Fort Worth.

Fort Worth *Mind.* 1933?–?. Weekly. Publisher: Raymond L. Melton and C. R. Wise. Fort Worth.

Forward Times. 1960–1977. Weekly. Publisher: Julius Carter. Editors: Allen Howard, Jan. 30, 1960–Dec. 2, 1961; Julius Carter, Dec. 9, l961–Dec. 31, 1967; Bud Johnson, Oct. 21, 1989. Houston. Continues as Houston *Forward Times.*

Free Man's Press. 1868. Weekly. Publisher: Free Man's Press Publishing Company. Austin.

Freedman's Press. July 18–25, 1868. Weekly. Publisher: Freedman's Press Publishing Company. Austin. Continues as *Free Man's Press.*

Freedman's Press. 1887–1891. Weekly. Editor: R. Nelson. Galveston.

Galveston *Examiner.* 1938–1940. Weekly. Publisher: B. M. Jackson. Galveston. Continues as *Examiner.*

Galveston *New Idea.* 1896–19??. Weekly. Galveston.

Galveston *Voice.* 1932?–. Weekly. Publisher: C. W. Rice. Editor: C. W. Rice. Galveston.

The Gold Dollar. 1876?–?. Frequency unknown. Publisher: Jacob Fontaine. Austin.

The Griot. 1980–1987?. Semiannual. Publisher: Southern Conference on Afro-American Studies. Editors: Shirley A. J. Hanshaw, 1980–Summer 1983; Ousseynou B. Traore, Winter 1984–Winter/Summer 1985 and Summer/Fall 1987; Andrew Baskin, Spring/Fall 1987. Houston.

Heart of Gospel Music Magazine. 1992–. Bimonthly. Publisher: Jacqueline Lloyd and Joann Armstrong. Editors: Jacqueline Lloyd and Joann Armstrong. Dallas.

Helping Hand. 1897?–19??. Monthly. Waco.

The Herald. 1927?–?. Frequency unknown. Publisher: Houston College for Negroes. Editor: Whitlowe R. Greene, Dec. 1933–May 1934. Houston.

The Herald. 1947–?. Monthly. Publisher: Texas State University. Editor: Martin Mayfield Jr., Dec. 1947–May 1948; Loyce E. Allen, Oct. 10, 1952. Houston.

Hip. 1976–1982. Monthly. Publisher: Beatrice Pringle. Editor: Edan K. Turner. Fort Worth.

Hoo-Doo. 1973–1980?. Frequency unknown. Publisher: Energy Earth Communications. Editor: Ahmos Zu-Bolton III. Galveston.

Houston *Call.* 1970?–?. Weekly. Publisher: Rev. Samuel Ammons. Houston.

Houston *Defender.* 1930–. Weekly. Publisher: Sonceria Messiah. Editor: Sonceria Messiah. Houston.

Houston *Forward Times.* 1977–. Weekly. Publisher: Forward Times Publishing Company. Houston. Continues *Forward Times.*

Houston *Informer.* 1919–1934?. Weekly. Publisher: C. F. Richardson. Houston. Continued by Houston *Informer and the Texas Freeman.*

Houston *Informer.* 1946?–195?. Weekly. Houston.

Houston *Newspages.* 1986–. Weekly. Publisher: Diana Fallis. Editor: Francis Page Sr. Houston.

Houston *Sun.* 1982–. Weekly. Publisher: DLR Publishing Company. Editor: Doris Ellis. Houston.

Illustrated News. 1923?–?. Weekly. Publisher: Rev. W. I. Solomon. Austin.

In Sepia. 1959?–?. Weekly. Publisher: Davis and Associates. Dallas.

The Independent. 1898–1905. Weekly. Publisher: Crawford and Osborne. Editor: Nannie R. Crawford. Houston.

Info/Line: Voice of the Minority Business Community. 1983?–. Quarterly. Publisher: Atukacon International. Editor: D. Raymon Moy. Dallas.

The Informer and Texas Freeman. 1934?–1971. Weekly. Publishers: Carter W. Wesley and Doris Wesley. 1971–1972. Daily. Publishers: James Watson, George McElroy. Editor: George McElroy. 1993. Weekly. Publishers: Lorenza Butler Jr., Pluria W. Marshall. Editor: George McElroy. Houston.

The Item. 1891–1900. Weekly. Publisher: J. G. Griffin, Ellis Willis. Dallas.

Jive. 1952?–?. Monthly. Publisher: Beatrice Pringle. Editor: Edna K. Turner. Fort Worth.

Key News. 1962–?. Weekly. Publisher: Al Smith. Editor: Al Smith. Dallas.

The Last Trump. 1991–. Six times a year. Publisher: Jeremiah Cummings, Donna Howard. Editor: Donna Howard. Arlington.

Lincoln Tiger-Gram. 1976–?. Biannual? Publisher: Lincoln High School. Editor: Dorothy M. Watson. Dallas.

Link. 1983?–?. Monthly. Dallas.

Lubbock *Digest.* 1977–1982. Biweekly. Publisher: Kathboband Associates. Lubbock. Continued by *Southwest Digest.*

Manhattan Heights and West Texas Times. 1966–1968. Weekly. Publisher: Norman L. Williamson. Lubbock. Continues *Manhattan Heights Times.* Continued by *West Texas Times.*

Manhattan Heights Times. 1961–1965. Weekly. Publisher: Scott and Norman Williamson. Lubbock. Continued by *Manhattan Heights and West Texas Times.*

Mary Allen News. 1929?–?. Biweekly. Publisher: Prairie View State College. Editor: Napoleon B. Edward, Oct. 1931–Jan. 1936. Prairie View.

The Pythias and Calanthean Review. Dates unknown. Quarterly. Dallas.

Rootsearching. 1977–1978?. Biweekly. Publisher: Marleta Childs. Editor: Marleta Childs. Lubbock.

San Antonio *Inquirer.* 1906-?. Weekly. Publisher: G. W. Bouldin, Nov. 29, 1924–. San Antonio.

San Antonio *Inquirer* (Gonzales section). 1924–?. Frequency unknown. Gonzales.

San Antonio *Register.* 1931–. Weekly. Publisher: Edward Glosson. San Antonio.

Senior's Weekly. Dates unknown. Weekly. Publisher: Senior Class of Dallas Colored High School. Editor: Duke L. Slaughter. Dallas.

Sepia. 1952–1982?. Monthly. Publisher: Beatrice Pringle. Fort Worth.

Shining Star. 1959–?. Weekly. Publisher: Callins Publishing Company. Editor: Mrs. Joe Callins. Taylor.

Silhouette. 1979?–?. Bimonthly. Publisher: Michael D. Buford. Bryan.

Smith County Herald. 1978–. Weekly. Publisher: Frances Pierce. Editor: Teresa Battles. Tyler.

Soul Confessions. 1975–?. Monthly. Publisher: Beatrice Pringle. Editor: Edna K. Turner. Fort Worth.

Soulteen. 1971?–1982?. Monthly. Publisher: Beatrice Pringle. Editor: Edna K. Turner. Fort Worth.

Southern Opportunity. 1926?–?. Monthly. Publisher: County Training School. Editor: F. W. Wheeler. Wortham.

Southwest Digest. 1982–?. Weekly. Publisher: Lubbock Digest Publishing Company. Lubbock. Continues Lubbock *Digest.*

Southwest Newsletter. 1975?–?. Irregular. Publisher: Museum of African American Life and Culture. Dallas.

Sunday School Herald. 1891–1892. Weekly. Publisher: L. L. Campbell. Austin.

Taborian Banner. 1905–?. Monthly. Publisher: W. Hartley Jackson. Galveston.

Tarrant County Black Historical and Genealogical Society Newsletter. 1982–. Irregular. Publisher: Tarrant County Black Historical and Genealogical Society. Editors: Mae Frances Leach Nolin, Sept. l987–Feb. 1988; Mary Barnett Curtis, June–Aug. 1982; Opal Lee, June–Aug. 1982. Fort Worth.

Terrellife. 1929?–?. Monthly. Publisher: I. M.

Terrell High School. Editors: Versia Cavanall, Mar. 21, 1935; Norma Jean Holloway, Mar. 28, 1943; Tom Smith, Nov. 20, 1944–Apr. 25, 1945; Don Simpkins, Nov. 21, 1945–May 27, 1946; Eli Davis, Nov. 27, 1946. Fort Worth.

Texarkana *Courier.* 1975–. Weekly. Publisher: Elridge Robertson. Editor: Ivy Jordan. Texarkana.

Texas Commission on Race Relations Newsletter. Dates unknown. Frequency unknown. Publisher: Southern Regional Council. Austin.

Texas Examiner. 1942?–?. Bimonthly. Publisher: Teachers State Association of Texas. Editors: Hazel Harvey Peace, Mar./Apr. 1948; Leslie J. White, Jan./Feb. 1956; Vernon McDaniel, Mar./Apr. 1960–Sept./Oct. 1962. Fort Worth.

Texas Freeman. 1893–1934?. Irregular. Publishers: C. N. Love, Emmett J. Scott, Jack Tibbitt. Houston.

Texas Interracial Review. 1940–1969. Semimonthly. Waco. Subsequently published in Austin by Mason Smith, 1941–1969. Merged with *Capital City Argus* to form *Capital City Argus and Interracial Review.*

Texas State University Herald. 1947?–?. Monthly. Publisher: Texas State University for Negroes. Houston.

Texas Steer. 1941–?. Monthly?. Publisher: Texas College. Editor: William H. Lathen. Tyler.

Texas Times. 1977–. Daily. Publisher: Woodie Webber. Editor: Mary Webber. Fort Worth.

The Tillotsonian. 1937–?. Monthly. Publisher: Tillotson College. Editor: Charles A. Stubblefield. Austin.

Times Review. 1968?–?. Frequency unknown. Dallas.

Torchlight Appeal. 1886–1893. Weekly. Editor: J. H. Milledge. Fort Worth.

Tribune. 1970?–?. Weekly. Austin.

USA Monitor. 1940–. Monthly. Publisher: William Howard Wilburn Sr., Earl L. Burell. Editor: William Howard Wilburn Sr. Fort Worth.

The Villager. 1973–. Weekly. Publisher: Tommy Wyatt. Editor: Tommy Wyatt. Austin.

Voice of Hope. 1968?–1975?. Weekly. Publisher: Voice of Hope Publishing. Editor: Earl E. Allen, May 22, 1971–April 20, 1974; George Leland, April 27, 1974–Jan. 24, 1975; Melva J. Becnel, Feb. 1–Mar. 29, 1975. Waco.

Waco *Good News.* 1880–?. Weekly. Publisher: James Horton. Waco.

Weekly Bulletin. 1901–?. Weekly. Publisher: Bulletin Publishing Company. Austin.

West Texas Times. Jan. 4, 1968–Dec. 26, 1979. Weekly. Publisher: Norman L. Williamson. Lubbock.

Western Star. 1893–1932. Weekly. Publisher: Western Star Publishing Company. Houston.

Wiley College Alumni Newsletter. 1975?–1976?. Frequency unknown. Publisher: Wiley College. Marshall.

Wiley Reporter. 1903?–?. Monthly. Publisher: Wiley College. Editors: Cleveland J. Gay, Dec. 1932; H. S. Mason, Jan. 1942; Mary Crawford, May 1945–Mar. 1947. Marshall.

The X-Ray. 1911–?. Weekly. Publisher: X-Ray Publishing Company. Fort Worth.

INDEX

(Photographs are indicated by boldfaced page numbers.)